READING QUEST

Raluca Hatinceanu

STARTER

A Faithful Guide Through
Your Reading Adventures

DARAKWON

Radu Hadrian Hotinceanu

- MFA degree in Creative Writing from Arizona State University
- BA degree in English & Rhetoric from State University of New York at Binghamton
- Professor of English Language and Literature at Seoul Women's University
- Over 20 years of teaching experience at universities in Korea
- Former English language editor of ASIANA In-flight Magazines, *SPACE* and *Diplomacy* magazines

READING QUEST STARTER

Author	Radu Hadrian Hotinceanu
Publisher	Chung Kyudo
Editors	Kim Taeyon, Cho Sangik
Designer	Hwang Sooyoung, Jang Meeyeoun
Photo Credits	pg. 32-33 (young couple) Elena Dijour / Shutterstock.com; pg. 35 (record shop) www.hollandfoto.net / Shutterstock.com; pg. 58 (app on a smartphone screen) bangoland / Shutterstock.com; pg. 82 (hotel) Patrick Horton / Shutterstock.com; pg. 83 (shoppers) Derick Hudson / Shutterstock.com; pg. 104-105 (Cristiano Ronaldo) Marco Iacobucci EPP / Shutterstock.com; pg. 106 (Above: Cristiano Ronaldo) bestino / Shutterstock.com, (Below: Cristiano Ronaldo) AGIF / Shutterstock.com; pg. 107 (bust of Cristiano Ronaldo) Matija Zupan / Shutterstock.com; pg. 109 (Cristiano Ronaldo) Oleksandr Osipov / Shutterstock.com; pg. 112-113 (Ralph Lauren) FashionStock.com / Shutterstock.com; pg. 114 (Ralph Lauren) FashionStock.com / Shutterstock.com; pg. 115 (models) FashionStock.com / Shutterstock.com; pg. 115 (Polo Ralph Lauren symbol) Usa-Pyon / Shutterstock.com; pg. 117 (Ralph Lauren) FashionStock.com / Shutterstock.com

First Published in May 2019
By Darakwon Inc.
Darakwon Bldg., 211, Munbal-ro, Paju-si, Gyeonggi-do 10881
Republic of Korea
Tel: 82-2-736-2031 (Ext. 552)

Price	15,000 won
ISBN	978-89-277-0970-1 14740
	978-89-277-0969-5 14740 (set)

www.darakwon.co.kr

Components	Main Book / Free MP3 Recordings Available Online

9 8 7 6 5 4 3   23 24 25 26 27

To the Readers

Reading Quest Starter is the first book in a three-book series of readers for adult learners of English. This series contains readings that range from a high-beginning to a high-advanced level. All three books in the series were written with the goal of presenting readings that are interesting, fun, and level appropriate.

Reading Quest Starter is divided into seven units that explore the topics of history, music, self-improvement, technology, science, travel, and people. Each unit presents two current and engaging stories on a topic. These reading passages are previewed in a Unit Preview section and are further explored in Reading Comprehension, Summarizing Information, Vocabulary in Context, and Reading Connections sections.

The discussion activities in the Unit Preview make this section ideal for classroom use. The Reading Comprehension section emphasizes the development of reading skills such as searching for details and identifying the main topic. The Summarizing Information section gives readers the chance to recall the main points of the reading passage through key vocabulary and through their own words. The Vocabulary in Context section focuses on word analysis skills such as determining the connotations of words and understanding the use of phrasal expressions. Lastly, the Reading Connections section provides further information that is relevant to the topic, giving readers the chance to extend their understanding of the reading passages.

Radu Hadrian Hotinceanu

CONTENTS

UNIT ELEMENTS

Each unit of *Reading Quest Starter* includes the following sections and features:

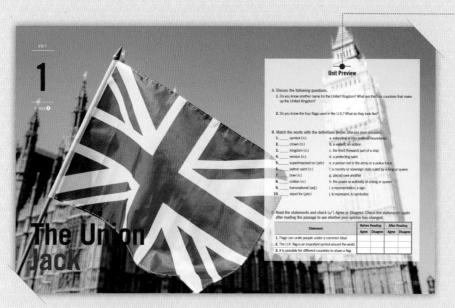

◀ Unit Preview
Three types of activities prepare readers for the reading passage. Readers can see how their thoughts have changed after reading the passage by using the anticipation guide table at the bottom.

◀ Tips
Tips on reading strategies that follow each reading passage introduce readers to practical ways to improve their reading skills.

Reading Passages ▶
Each reading passage has the appropriate sentence length and complexity for the high-beginning to low-intermediate level.

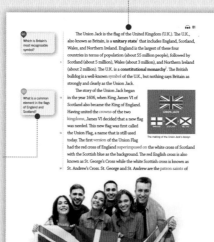

Quick Questions ▶
Quick questions are provided in the margins of each reading passage to encourage readers to consider their comprehension of the passage's details while reading.

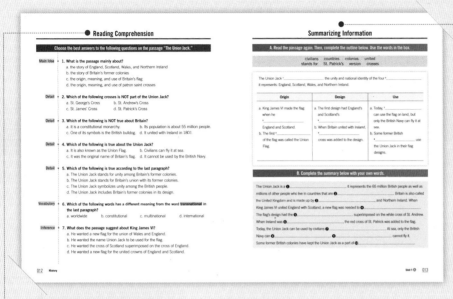

◀ Summarizing Information

Fill-in-the-blank summary exercises reinforce readers' comprehension of main points and key vocabulary in the reading passage.

◀ Reading Comprehension

A set of comprehension questions helps readers test their understanding of the key information in the reading passage.

◀ Reading Connections

Every unit includes an additional reading on a topic related to the unit's reading passage. It extends readers' knowledge and provides them with the opportunity for further reflection on the subject.

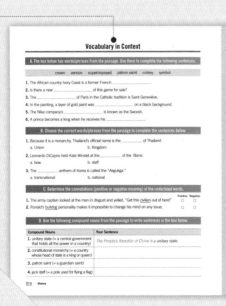

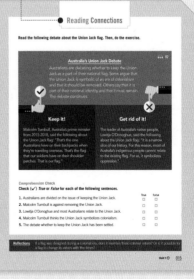

Vocabulary in Context ▶

Different types of vocabulary exercises provide practice in using the unit's vocabulary in practical contexts.

1

The Union Jack

Unit Preview

A. Discuss the following questions.

1. Do you know another name for the United Kingdom? What are the four countries that make up the United Kingdom?

2. Do you know the four flags used in the UK? What do they look like?

B. Match the words with the definitions below. Discuss your answers.

1. _____ symbol (*n.*)

2. _____ crown (*n.*)

3. _____ kingdom (*n.*)

4. _____ version (*n.*)

5. _____ superimposed on (*phr.*)

6. _____ patron saint (*n.*)

7. _____ bow (*n.*)

8. _____ civilian (*n.*)

9. _____ transnational (*adj.*)

10. _____ stand for (*phr.*)

a. extending across national boundaries

b. a variant; an edition

c. the front (forward) part of a ship

d. a protecting saint

e. a person not in the army or a police force

f. a country or sovereign state ruled by a king or queen

g. placed over another

h. the power or authority of a king or queen

i. a representation; a sign

j. to represent; to symbolize

C. Read the statements and check (✓) *Agree* or *Disagree*. Check the statements again after reading the passage to see whether your opinion has changed.

Statement	Before Reading		After Reading	
	Agree	Disagree	Agree	Disagree
1. Flags can unite people under a common ideal.				
2. The UK flag is an important symbol around the world.				
3. It is possible for different countries to share a flag.				

Q1

Which is Britain's most recognizable symbol?

Q2

What is a common element in the flags of England and Scotland?

The Union Jack is the flag of the United Kingdom (UK). The UK, also known as Britain, is a **unitary state**[1] that includes England, Scotland, Wales, and Northern Ireland. England is the largest of these four countries in terms of population (about 55 million people), followed by Scotland
5   (about 5 million), Wales (about 3 million), and Northern Ireland (about 2 million). The UK is a **constitutional monarchy**[2]. The British bulldog is a well-known symbol of the UK, but nothing says Britain as strongly and clearly as the Union Jack.

The story of the Union Jack began
10   in the year 1606, when King James VI of Scotland also became the King of England. Having united the crowns of the two kingdoms, James VI decided that a new flag was needed. This new flag was first called
15   the Union Flag, a name that is still used today. The first version of the Union Flag

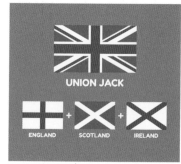

The making of the Union Jack's design

had the red cross of England superimposed on the white cross of Scotland with the Scottish blue as the background. The red English cross is also known as St. George's Cross while the white Scottish cross is known as
20   St. Andrew's Cross. St. George and St. Andrew are the patron saints of

England and Scotland, respectively.

When Britain united with Ireland in 1801, the red cross of St. Patrick, the patron saint of Ireland, was included in the Union Jack. This thinner red cross can be seen running along the white Scottish cross. The design was kept even after the southern part of Ireland gained independence from Britain in 1921.

The name of Union Jack is synonymous with the name Union Flag, and it comes from the flag's use at sea. It is customary for ships to fly their national flags, usually at the bow, attached to the **jack staff**[3]. The flag was therefore called the Union Jack. Today, the Union Jack can be used by civilians on land, but only the British Navy can fly the flag at sea. Merchant ships are not allowed to fly the Union Jack.

The Union Jack is included in the flags of four of Britain's former colonies: Australia, New Zealand, Tuvalu, and Fiji. The Union Jack is therefore a transnational flag. It represents not only the British union but also a family of nations: Britain's former colonies. The Union Jack stands for unity among the people of Britain and for harmony between Britain and its former colonies.

The flag of Australia with the Union Jack in the top left corner

---

TIP

Focus Your Attention on the Reading

Do you want to read faster? Do you want to increase your understanding of what you are reading? Start by forming a very simple but extremely important habit: Focus strictly on your reading. You probably need a quiet place, such as a corner table in a quiet café. You also need to become a more attentive, active reader. Reading is not like watching TV—something done in a passive manner. Reading requires mental effort, and you must make that effort when you read. Give 100% of your concentration every time you read, and in time you will become a better reader. Don't be distracted by the scenes outside the café, by thoughts of your friends, or by text messages on your phone. It is a good idea to turn off your phone when you are reading.

---

1   **unitary state** a state where the central government holds all the power over the members of the state. More than 150 countries in the world have this type of political system. The U.S. is a federal state, where the power is shared among the 50 American states in the American union.

2   **constitutional monarchy** a form of government where the monarch (a king or queen) has certain authority as defined by the constitution. Some monarchs (the Japanese and Swedish kings) have no real powers while others (the Moroccan and Saudi kings) have significant powers.

3   **jack staff** the name of a pole mounted on the bow of a ship on which a flag is flown.

Reading Comprehension

Main Idea

1. What is the passage mainly about?
a. the story of England, Scotland, Wales, and Northern Ireland
b. the story of Britain's former colonies
c. the origin, meaning, and use of Britain's flag
d. the origin, meaning, and use of patron saint crosses

Detail

2. Which of the following crosses is NOT part of the Union Jack?
a. St. George's Cross
b. St. Andrew's Cross
c. St. James' Cross
d. St. Patrick's Cross

Detail

3. Which of the following is NOT true about Britain?
a. It is a constitutional monarchy.
b. Its population is about 55 million people.
c. One of its symbols is the British bulldog.
d. It united with Ireland in 1801.

Detail

4. Which of the following is true about the Union Jack?
a. It is also known as the Union Flag.
b. Civilians can fly it at sea.
c. It was the original name of Britain's flag.
d. It cannot be used by the British Navy.

Detail

5. Which of the following is true according to the last paragraph?
a. The Union Jack stands for unity among Britain's former colonies.
b. The Union Jack stands for Britain's union with its former colonies.
c. The Union Jack symbolizes unity among the British people.
d. The Union Jack includes Britain's former colonies in its design.

Vocabulary

6. Which of the following words has a different meaning from the word transnational in the last paragraph?
a. worldwide
b. constitutional
c. multinational
d. international

Inference

7. What does the passage suggest about King James VI?
a. He wanted a new flag for the union of Wales and England.
b. He wanted the name Union Jack to be used for the flag.
c. He wanted the cross of Scotland superimposed on the cross of England.
d. He wanted a new flag for the united crowns of England and Scotland.

Summarizing Information

A. Read the passage again. Then, complete the outline below. Use the words in the box.

civilians	countries	colonies	united
stands for	St. Patrick's	version	crosses

The Union Jack [1]_____ the unity and national identity of the four [2]_____ it represents: England, Scotland, Wales, and Northern Ireland.

Origin	Design	Use
a. King James VI made the flag when he [3]_____ England and Scotland.	a. The first design had England's and Scotland's [5]_____.	a. Today, [7]_____ can use the flag on land, but only the British Navy can fly it at sea.
b. The first [4]_____ of the flag was called the Union Flag.	b. When Britain united with Ireland, [6]_____ cross was added to the design.	b. Some former British [8]_____ use the Union Jack in their flag designs.

B. Complete the summary below with your own words.

The Union Jack is a ❶_____. It represents the 65 million British people as well as

millions of other people who live in countries that are ❷_____. Britain is also called

the United Kingdom and is made up of ❸_____, and Northern Ireland. When

King James VI united England with Scotland, a new flag was needed to ❹_____.

The flag's design had the ❺_____ superimposed on the white cross of St. Andrew.

When Ireland was ❻_____, the red cross of St. Patrick was added to the flag.

Today, the Union Jack can be used by civilians ❼_____. At sea, only the British

Navy can ❽_____. ❾_____ cannot fly it.

Some former British colonies have kept the Union Jack as a part of ❿_____.

Vocabulary in Context

A. The box below has words/phrases from the passage. Use them to complete the following sentences.

crown   version   superimposed   patron saint   colony   symbol

1. The African country Ivory Coast is a former French ....

2. Is there a new .... of this game for sale?

3. The .... of Paris in the Catholic tradition is Saint Geneviève.

4. In the painting, a layer of gold paint was .... on a black background.

5. The Nike company's .... is known as the Swoosh.

6. A prince becomes a king when he receives his ....

B. Choose the correct words/phrases from the passage to complete the sentences below.

1. Because it is a monarchy, Thailand's official name is the .... of Thailand.

    a. Union   b. Kingdom

2. Leonardo DiCaprio held Kate Winslet at the .... of the *Titanic*.

    a. bow   b. staff

3. The .... anthem of Korea is called the "Aegukga."

    a. transnational   b. national

C. Determine the connotation (positive or negative meaning) of the underlined words.

	Positive	Negative
1. The army captain looked at the man in disgust and yelled, "Get this civilian out of here!"	☐	☐
2. Ronald's bulldog personality makes it impossible to change his mind on any issue.	☐	☐

D. Use the following compound nouns from the passage to write sentences in the box below.

Compound Nouns	Your Sentence
1. unitary state (= a central government that holds all the power in a country)	*The People's Republic of China is a **unitary state**.*
2. constitutional monarchy (= a country whose head of state is a king or queen)	
3. patron saint (= a guardian saint)	
4. jack staff (= a pole used for flying a flag)	

Reading Connections

Read the following debate about the Union Jack flag. Then, do the exercise.

Australia's Union Jack Debate

🎧 02

Australians are debating whether to keep the Union Jack as a part of their national flag. Some argue that the Union Jack is symbolic of an era of colonialism and that it should be removed. Others say that it is part of their national identity and that it must remain. The debate continues.

Keep it!

Malcolm Turnbull, Australia's prime minister from 2015-2018, said the following about the Union Jack flag: "That's the one Australians have on their backpacks when they're traveling overseas. That's the flag that our soldiers have on their shoulder patches. That is our flag."

Get rid of it!

The leader of Australia's native people, Lowitja O'Donoghue, said the following about the Union Jack flag: "It is a narrow slice of our history. For this reason, most of Australia's indigenous people cannot relate to the existing flag. For us, it symbolizes oppression."

Comprehension Check

Check (✓) *True* or *False* for each of the following sentences.

	True	False
1. Australians are divided on the issue of keeping the Union Jack.	☐	☐
2. Malcolm Turnbull is against removing the Union Jack.	☐	☐
3. Lowitja O'Donoghue and most Australians relate to the Union Jack.	☐	☐
4. Malcolm Turnbull thinks the Union Jack symbolizes colonialism.	☐	☐
5. The debate whether to keep the Union Jack has been settled.	☐	☐

Reflections   If a flag was designed during a colonial era, does it maintain those colonial values? Or is it possible for a flag to change its values with the times?

Miss
Unsinkable

Unit Preview

A. Discuss the following questions.

1. What was the *Titanic*? How did it sink? Was there another ship like the *Titanic* built?

2. Did the *Titanic* sinking have any survivors? Have you heard of Violet Jessop?

B. Match the words with the definitions below. Discuss your answers.

1. _____ scores of (*phr.*)   a. a large number of

2. _____ defy (*v.*)   b. unimportant; of little value

3. _____ streak of luck (*phr.*)   c. bad luck

4. _____ hire (*v.*)   d. to hit

5. _____ strike (*v.*)   e. lucky

6. _____ fortunate (*adj.*)   f. repeatedly; on many occasions

7. _____ propeller (*n.*)   g. a spinning shaft with two or more blades

8. _____ misfortune (*n.*)   h. to refuse to obey; to resist

9. _____ trivial (*adj.*)   i. a continuous period of luck or fortune

10. _____ time and again (*phr.*)   j. to give a job to someone

C. Read the statements and check (✓) *Agree* or *Disagree*. Check the statements again after reading the passage to see whether your opinion has changed.

Statement	Before Reading		After Reading	
	Agree	Disagree	Agree	Disagree
1. There is no such thing as a miracle.				
2. Some people are luckier than others.				
3. You have to overcome your fears to live a full life.				

03

Throughout history, there have been scores of people who have avoided tragedy thanks to some unbelievable luck. The story of Violet Jessop is perhaps the most fascinating example of defying fate with a streak of luck.

Q1

Jessop's lucky streak started early in life. What was her first chance of luck?

5

Violet Constance Jessop was born in Argentina in 1887. She was the oldest of nine children, so she spent most of her childhood taking care of her younger siblings. During her childhood, Jessop became very ill with **tuberculosis (TB)**[1], which she miraculously survived.

Violet Constance Jessop

10

Jessop's father died when she was 16, so her mother took a job as a stewardess on a cruise ship to support the family. In 1908, at the age of 21, Jessop herself took a stewardess position aboard the ship *Orinoco*.

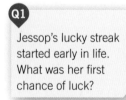

15

Two years later, Jessop was hired aboard the *Olympic*, the sister ship of *Britannic* and the famous *Titanic*, all three of which belonged to the White Star Line. The following year, the *Olympic* collided with the British warship *Hawke*. Both ships were damaged in the collision, but fortunately they did not sink and there were no deaths.

Titanic's sister ship, the hospital ship *Britannic*

As the *Olympic* underwent repairs, Jessop took a job aboard the *Titanic*. On April 14, 1912, just four days after Jessop began her new job, the *Titanic* struck an iceberg. The *Titanic's* officers ordered her to go into lifeboat No. 16 to show the passengers how to behave in the lifeboat. <u>This fortunate need</u> to demonstrate to the passengers how to act in an emergency saved her life.

The iceberg suspected of having sunk the *Titanic*

The last lifeboat being launched from the *Titanic*

After two accidents at sea, most people would not go near a ship again. But not Jessop. During World War I, she served as a Red Cross stewardess aboard the hospital ship *Britannic*. The *Britannic* was transporting injured soldiers to the United Kingdom when it hit a German mine in the **Aegean Sea**[2] and sank. Once again, Jessop found herself in a lifeboat. But this time, the lifeboat was almost sucked in by the sinking ship's propellers. Jessop had to jump into the water to survive. Good luck, it seems, was still on her side.

For some reason, every misfortune that fate threw at Violet Jessop, from tuberculosis to a German mine, seemed trivial next to her good luck. She proved fate time and again to be unsinkable. So after World War I, in 1920, Violet Jessop naturally returned to work for the White Star Line.

20

25

30

35

40

Q2

Jessop twice found herself in a lifeboat. Would you consider her an optimist or a pessimist?

TIP

Preview the Reading

Good readers have a habit of previewing their readings. This allows them to improve their reading comprehension. Previewing can take between 30-60 seconds. This is what you can do for all your reading passages: 1. Look at the title, pictures, captions, and words marked in bold letters or italics. 2. Glance at the first and last paragraphs, including the first sentences of these paragraphs. 3. Ask yourself, "What is this passage about?" After you come up with an answer, you are ready to start reading in a detailed, focused way.

---

1   **tuberculosis (TB)** a disease of the lungs caused by the *tuberculosis* bacteria
2   **Aegean Sea** a body of water in the Mediterranean Sea, near Greece

Reading Comprehension

Main Idea

1. **What is the passage mainly about?**
   a. the unsinkable ships of the White Star Line
   b. the misfortunate fates of the *Titanic* and *Britannic*
   c. the childhood and jobs of Violet Jessop
   d. Violet Jessop's streak of luck throughout life

Reference

2. **What does the phrase <u>this fortunate need</u> in paragraph 4 refer to?**
   a. the need to obey the *Titanic*'s officers
   b. the need to have a job at White Star Line
   c. the need to assist the passengers
   d. the need to have the *Olympic* repaired

Detail

3. **Which of the following ships underwent repairs after a collision?**
   a. *Titanic*   b. *Olympic*   c. *Orinoco*   d. *Britannic*

Detail

4. **Which of the following is NOT true according to the passage?**
   a. Violet Jessop had eight siblings.
   b. Violet Jessop's mother worked as a stewardess on a cruise ship.
   c. The *Olympic*, the *Titanic*, and the *Britannic* were all sister ships.
   d. The *Titanic* sank in the Aegean Sea.

Vocabulary

5. **Which of the following words is unrelated to the others?**
   a. sink   b. collide   c. strike   d. hit

Inference

6. **What does the phrase "but not Jessop" in paragraph 5 suggest about Violet Jessop's character?**
   a. She was bold.   b. She was outgoing.
   c. She was hesitant.   d. She was cheerful.

Inference

7. **What can be inferred from the last paragraph about fate?**
   a. It made Violet Jessop return to White Star Line.
   b. It allowed Violet Jessop to survive World War I.
   c. It was insignificant compared to Violet Jessop's luck.
   d. It is trivial compared to other things in life.

Summarizing Information

A. Read the passage again. Then, complete the outline below. Use the words in the box.

| aboard | tuberculosis | propellers | survived |
| iceberg | tragedy | struck | mine | ordered |

Violet Jessop avoided ¹ _____ throughout her life thanks to some unbelievable luck. She was born in a large family in Argentina, where she overcame ² _____ as a child. She also ³ _____ two disasters on ships belonging to White Star Line.

Olympic	Titanic	Britannic
a. Jessop was hired ⁴ _____ the *Olympic* in 1910.	a. The *Titanic* struck an ⁶ _____ in 1912.	a. The *Britannic* struck a ⁸ _____ in the Aegean Sea.
b. The *Olympic* ⁵ _____ the *HMS Hawke*, but there were no deaths.	b. Jessop was ⁷ _____ into a lifeboat, which saved her life.	b. Jessop jumped into the water to escape the sinking ship's ⁹ _____ .

B. Complete the summary below with your own words.

Violet Jessop was born in Argentina, where she spent most of her childhood taking care of her
❶ _____ . While still a child, she ❷ _____ ,
a very dangerous disease of the lungs. In 1908, at the age of 21, Jessop was hired to work
❸ _____ on the *Orinoco*. Two years later, while working aboard the *Olympic*,
Jessop saw ❹ _____ with the British warship *HMS Hawke*. Her next job was
❺ _____ , which was *Olympic*'s sister ship. The *Titanic*
❻ _____ and sank, but Jessop ❼ _____ . Jessop took her
next job aboard the ❽ _____ *Britannic*. Amazingly, she survived another sinking after
the *Britannic* ❾ _____ . Throughout her life, Violet Jessop was fortunate to have a
❿ _____ that saved her from a number of tragic events.

Vocabulary in Context

A. The box below has words/phrases from the passage. Use them to complete the following sentences.

| hired | strike | fate | take | scores of | misfortune |

1. Jenny had the _____ of breaking her leg while skiing.
2. Some people believe that they cannot escape their _____ in life.
3. As soon as he was _____, he invited all of his friends over for a celebration.
4. Joey's plan was to _____ a bartending job while studying at his university.
5. _____ tourists visit the Louvre Museum this time of the year.
6. Here are the keys to my car, but please try not to _____ anyone on the road.

B. Choose the correct words/phrases from the passage to complete the sentences below.

1. Early in his 20s, Louie was _____ to get a job at the Unicorn Tech Company.
   a. fortunate
   b. hired

2. Richard spends a lot of his free time _____ his two dogs.
   a. defying
   b. taking care of

3. Lisa _____ as a sales manager for many years before moving to the Marketing Department.
   a. behaved
   b. served

C. Determine the connotation (positive or negative meaning) of the underlined words.

	Positive	Negative
1. Larry spent most of his life focusing on <u>trivial</u> problems and missed the larger picture.	☐	☐
2. The woman <u>defied</u> convention and lived life on her own terms.	☐	☐

D. Use the following phrases from the passage to write sentences in the box below.

Phrases	Your Sentence
1. streak of luck (= a continuous period of luck)	*It seems James Bond always has a **streak of luck** at casinos.*
2. scores of (= a large number of)	
3. time and again (= repeatedly)	
4. on one's side (= helping someone)	

Reading Connections

Read the following notes from Violet Jessop's memoirs. Then, do the exercises.

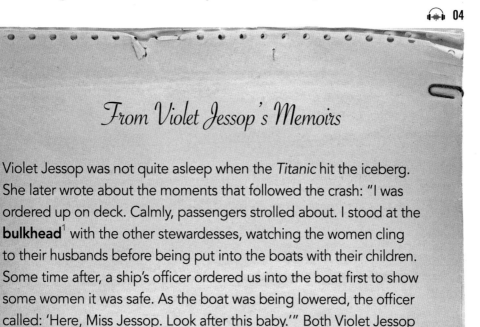

04

From Violet Jessop's Memoirs

Violet Jessop was not quite asleep when the *Titanic* hit the iceberg. She later wrote about the moments that followed the crash: "I was ordered up on deck. Calmly, passengers strolled about. I stood at the **bulkhead**[1] with the other stewardesses, watching the women cling to their husbands before being put into the boats with their children. Some time after, a ship's officer ordered us into the boat first to show some women it was safe. As the boat was being lowered, the officer called: 'Here, Miss Jessop. Look after this baby.'" Both Violet Jessop and the baby survived the *Titanic* tragedy.

---

1   **bulkhead** a dividing wall between compartments on a ship or airplane

Comprehension Check

Check (✓) *True* or *False* for each of the following sentences.

	True	False
1. Jessop was sleeping when the *Titanic* hit the iceberg.	☐	☐
2. After the crash, Jessop received an order to go up to the deck.	☐	☐
3. Jessop watched the husbands being put into boats.	☐	☐
4. She was ordered into a boat to show the women it was safe.	☐	☐
5. Jessop and the ship officer both survived the tragedy.	☐	☐

Reflections   Violet Jessop's story shows us her loyalty to the company that employed her: the White Star Line. After surviving the sinking of two of its ships, she went right back to work. These days, loyalty is quickly disappearing from the workplace for both employees and employers. Is the disappearance of workplace loyalty a good thing or bad thing?

The Age of AI Music Composers

Unit Preview

A. Discuss the following questions.

1. Do you believe that creativity only belongs to humans? Or are there other sources of creativity in our world?

2. Do you think that creativity can be learned? Or is it a talent that we are born with?

B. Match the words with the definitions below. Discuss your answers.

1. _____ bring to mind (*phr.*)
2. _____ piece (*n.*)
3. _____ artificial (*adj.*)
4. _____ undeniable (*adj.*)
5. _____ century (*n.*)
6. _____ chord (*n.*)
7. _____ collaborate (*v.*)
8. _____ replicate (*v.*)
9. _____ all on one's own (*phr.*)
10. _____ tune (*n.*)

a. a group of notes played together
b. made by humans; not natural
c. to copy; to repeat
d. to remind
e. a melody
f. a composition; a creation
g. a period of 100 years
h. to work together to produce something
i. beyond doubt; unquestionable
j. all by oneself; without help

C. Read the statements and check (✓) *Agree* or *Disagree*. Check the statements again after reading the passage to see whether your opinion has changed.

Statement	Before Reading		After Reading	
	Agree	Disagree	Agree	Disagree
1. AI (artificial intelligence) machines can learn to become creative.				
2. Future AI machines will replace human composers.				
3. AI machines are already writing original songs.				

05

The name Ludwig brings to mind the great German composer Ludwig van Beethoven, who wrote nine symphonies, six concertos, and a variety of other pieces of classical music. Beethoven's genius is undeniable. Almost two centuries after his death, his music and name remain popular throughout the world. Few people, however, know that Ludwig is also the name of an AI (artificial intelligence) music composer. Ludwig represents the increasing use of AI machines in fields that have traditionally required human talent.

Q1

How does the AI composer Ludwig help humans write music?

Ludwig is actually a software program that can help human music composers write songs. The human composer can upload a basic melody and choose a musical style, and Ludwig will add the chords and write all the parts of a full band. Ludwig is the perfect aid for human composers who are suffering from **writer's block**[1]. While Ludwig collaborates with human composers, there are AI music composers that create music all on their own.

Q2

How does Sony's AI composer write music?

Sony's Flow Machines project, for example, has developed an AI program that can compose professional-quality music. This complex AI composer was given the task of analyzing and identifying certain musical patterns in 15,000 songs. The AI composer is able to imitate the patterns it has identified, as well as change them to create its own original music.

Sony's AI composer does not know the basic rules of music or any music theory. Still, this did not stop it from releasing its first single, "Daddy's Car," a song that reminds some of a Beatles tune.

In contrast, AIVA Technologies, a company based in Luxembourg, trained its AI music composer AIVA in classical music theory. AIVA can create hundreds of hours of background classical music for different uses: computer games, shopping malls, and even orchestras. Perhaps due to its classical music training, AIVA was recognized by the Society of Authors, Composers, and Publishers of Music (SACEM).

AI software such as Ludwig can lead us to question whether talent is real. Listening to Beethoven's "Symphony No. 9" and AIVA's "Symphonic Ouverture in A Minor, Op. 23: Let'z Make It Happen," you realize that talent does exist, and it is not the machine that has it. Let's not forget that Beethoven was also a pianist who performed his own music. And when it comes to performance, there is no machine that comes close to replicating human talent. Still, future AI music composers may surprise us. After all, Ludwig can only get better with age, and unlike humans, it has an unlimited lifetime to improve.

A robotic arm playing a piano

TIP

Write Notes Instead of Highlighting

Using a highlighter is a good habit for improving your reading skills. You usually highlight new words, difficult sentences, and ideas. But it is possible to forget the reason you highlighted a certain text in the first place. Writing notes on the side of the text (annotating) is much more useful. As you write definitions of new words or phrases, explain a difficult idea in your own words, or make connections between different ideas (again, in your own words), your understanding of the text will increase. And all these notes will be there the next time you read the text, just in case you forget something. Here is an example of a note you can write for the last paragraph of the passage "The Age of AI Music Composers": I must listen to AIVA's "Symphonic Ouverture" to see if the comparison with Beethoven's "Symphony No. 9" is true!

---

1   **writer's block** the condition of being unable to think of what to write; a creativity block

Reading Comprehension

Main Idea

1. What is the passage mainly about?
- a. AI composers that can create or help humans create original music
- b. AI composers that have the human talent to create music
- c. AI composers that perform music as well as humans
- d. AI composers that show that human talent is not real

Detail

2. What does the name Ludwig refer to?
- a. a Flow Machines project
- b. an AI machine that writes original music
- c. a software program
- d. a current human music composer

Detail

3. Which of the following is true about Sony's AI music composer?
- a. It memorized 15,000 songs.
- b. It was trained in classical music.
- c. It collaborates with human composers.
- d. It wrote "Daddy's Car."

Detail

4. Which of the following is NOT true about AIVA?
- a. It can create background classical music.
- b. It can create computer games.
- c. It was trained in classical music theory.
- d. It was recognized by SACEM.

Vocabulary

5. Which of the following words has a different meaning from the others?
- a. composer
- b. song
- c. single
- d. tune

Inference

6. What can be inferred from the passage?
- a. AI composers can now replicate human talent.
- b. AI composers cannot replicate human talent yet.
- c. AI composers will never be able to replicate human talent.
- d. Human talent does not exist.

Inference

7. What does the passage suggest about the future?
- a. AI composers will improve.
- b. Human composers will improve.
- c. AI composers will have a limited lifetime.
- d. Humans will have an unlimited lifetime.

Summarizing Information

creates   trained   writer's block   imitates
AI machines   chords   musical patterns

¹_____ such as Ludwig, Sony's AI composer, and AIVA are helping human composers make music or composing original music.

The Ludwig AI Composer	Sony's AI Composer	The AIVA AI Composer
a. Helps human composers suffering from ²_____ b. Adds ³_____ to a chosen melody	a. Analyzed ⁴_____ in 15,000 songs b. ⁵_____ patterns and creates original music	a. Was ⁶_____ in classical music theory b. ⁷_____ background classical music

B. Complete the summary below with your own words.

❶_____ machines are now working in fields that require creativity, such as music composition. AI composers such as Ludwig can help human composers ❷_____. This is especially useful for human composers who ❸_____. Sony's AI composer can create its ❹_____. It already released a single that reminds people of ❺_____. The AIVA AI composer creates ❻_____ for shopping malls, ❼_____, and orchestras. Because of its classical music training, it ❽_____ by SACEM. Even though today's AI machines cannot ❾_____ humans, anything is possible in the future. AI composers like Ludwig can only ❿_____.

Vocabulary in Context

A. The box below has words/phrases from the passage. Use them to complete the following sentences.

| artificial | pieces | undeniable | lifetime | tune | all on his own |

1. The _____ on the radio is from my high school days.

2. Rachmaninoff's "Piano Concerto No. 3" is one of the most difficult classical _____ to play.

3. The stream that flows through downtown is _____, so it can be easily controlled.

4. My brother learned to speak three languages fluently _____.

5. Mary would need more than a _____ to improve her acting skills.

6. Mark's passion for animals is _____; he always volunteers at the animal shelter.

B. Choose the correct words/phrases from the passage to complete the sentences below.

1. Humans have _____ computers in the past to solve many problems.

   a. collaborated with   b. replicated

2. John's _____ is preventing him from finishing his new novel.

   a. creativity   b. writer's block

3. At the end of the day, I pick up a guitar and strum a few _____.

   a. patterns   b. chords

C. Determine the connotation (positive or negative meaning) of the underlined words.

	Positive	Negative
1. These days, many local musicians <u>replicate</u> songs they have heard abroad.	☐	☐
2. Joe's dad had a <u>talent</u> for crime. He was arrested a few times in his life.	☐	☐

D. Use the following verbs / phrasal verbs from the passage to write sentences in the box below.

Verbs / Phrasal Verbs	Your Sentence
1. replicate (= to copy; to repeat)	*It is very difficult for machines to **replicate** the human voice.*
2. collaborate (= to work together)	
3. bring to mind (= to remind)	

Read the following news release. Then, do the exercises.

🎧 06

In the News

Spotify's Robots Have a New Guru

Francois Pachet, a leading artificial intelligence researcher, has been hired by the popular online music streaming provider Spotify to help its AI music composers become more creative. Pachet will do his work at the company's Creator Technology Research Lab in Paris. Presently, Spotify has to pay royalties to human music composers each time one of their songs is streamed. In the future, it may not have to pay royalties if the music on its playlists is written by its own AI composers. There is a long way to go until AI composers can write hit songs, but Pachet and other researchers are already hard at work to ensure that day will come sooner rather than later.

Comprehension Check

Check (✓) *True* or *False* for each of the following sentences.

	True	False
1. Spotify is a popular online music streaming provider.	☐	☐
2. Francois Pachet has been hired by AI music composers in Paris.	☐	☐
3. Spotify pays royalties to human music composers.	☐	☐
4. Spotify will have to pay royalties to its AI music composers.	☐	☐
5. Spotify's AI composers are now writing hit songs with Pachet's help.	☐	☐

Reflections Machines are already replacing people in the manufacturing and service fields. Artificial intelligence is accelerating this trend and allowing machines to replace humans in other fields, such as the arts. In a future world of AI painters, composers, and interior designers, will humans be in danger of losing touch with their own creativity?

A Return to Vinyl

Unit Preview

A. Discuss the following questions.

1. Have you ever heard a vinyl record being played on a turntable? If so, was it in your home or somewhere else?

2. Do you own or have you ever owned a vinyl record? Or have you seen one at someone else's house? If so, what is or was the name of the album?

B. Match the words with the definitions below. Discuss your answers.

1. _____ comeback (*n.*)
2. _____ hipster (*n.*)
3. _____ turntable (*n.*)
4. _____ boom (*n.*)
5. _____ flip through (*phr.*)
6. _____ (record) sleeve (*n.*)
7. _____ admire (*v.*)
8. _____ pristine (*adj.*)
9. _____ fed up (*adj.*)
10. _____ crave (*v.*)

a. to regard someone or something with respect
b. to search or look quickly for something
c. clean as new; spotless
d. rapid growth
e. to feel a strong desire for something
f. a machine that plays vinyl records
g. a return to being a trend or fashion
h. a protective cover made of paper or cardboard
i. tired of or annoyed with a situation
j. a person who follows the latest trends or fashions

C. Read the statements and check (✓) *Agree* or *Disagree*. Check the statements again after reading the passage to see whether your opinion has changed.

Statement	Before Reading		After Reading	
	Agree	Disagree	Agree	Disagree
1. Only older people still listen to vinyl records.				
2. Vinyl records are cheaper than streamed albums.				
3. Vinyl records sound better than CDs and MP3s.				

Q1

Who are some of the people buying vinyl records?

Put away your VR glasses for a minute. Here is some old-school news for you: Vinyl is making a comeback. Blame it on the hipsters, or blame it on the **Baby Boomers**[1] or **Generation Xers**[2] who are feeling nostalgic about the turntable. The fact is that sales of vinyl records are enjoying a

5　global boom. But the return to vinyl is not just about nostalgia. It is also about collecting a piece of art, and ultimately it is about music that simply sounds better.

Those who feel nostalgic about vinyl miss the whole experience of owning records. They miss the time spent in music shops flipping through

10　rows of records to find the right one. They miss looking at the artwork on the sleeves of purchased records for hours. And they miss carefully lowering the needle onto the record and watching it spin while it plays their favorite music.

15　Then there are the vinyl collectors. These are the people who own records as

A turntable playing a vinyl record

pieces of art. They want a part of the musicians they admire, not just streamed songs on their computer. Price is not important to them. After all, the price of one vinyl record is about the same as a one-year subscription to Apple Music's library of 40 million songs. Some vinyl collectors do not even have turntables. And many vinyl collectors who have turntables do not even open their records to play them. Instead, they preserve them in pristine condition and proudly display them in their homes.

A vinyl record shop

But mostly, those who are returning to vinyl are fed up with the ultra-clean sound of digital music. They crave the warm, rich sound that a high-quality turntable can produce. And music lovers are not the only ones craving the vinyl sound. Indie bands such as Arctic Monkeys, the Strokes, and the White Stripes have been recording their music solely on vinyl records. They too are in love with the deep, rich, analog sound.

Q2
What is the main reason people are returning to vinyl?

In 2018, over 10 million vinyl records were sold in the U.S., which is almost a 20% increase from the previous year. What is more is that people of all ages are returning to vinyl. This is a reminder to all of us that quality should not be abandoned or replaced by technologies that promise more speed or higher quantities. Perhaps this is a nostalgic point of view, but if we are getting nostalgic about great sound, then maybe technology has been taking us in the wrong direction.

TIP

Use Chunking to Increase Reading Speed and Comprehension

Chunking is a reading strategy that allows your eyes to see multiple words, including entire phrases and short sentences, at one time instead of just individual words. This method of reading helps your brain recognize familiar patterns, thus increasing your reading speed and comprehension level. Let's look at an example of chunking for the second sentence of the passage "A Return to Vinyl." The sentence can be divided into the following chunks: 1. Blame it on the hipsters; 2. or blame it on the Baby Boomers or Generation Xers; 3. who are feeling nostalgic about the turntable. We divided the chunks at the first natural pause (the comma) and before the relative clause that describes the two generations. So when you read this sentence by using the chunking method, your eyes should stop only at the comma, before the "who," and at the period. You should not stop after every word. With enough practice, you will become more comfortable with chunking, and your reading speed and comprehension will increase accordingly.

---

1   **Baby Boomers** people born between 1946 and 1964
2   **Generation Xers** the generation that followed the Baby Boomers. People in this generation were born between 1965 and 1980.

Reading Comprehension

Choose the best answers to the following questions on the passage "A Return to Vinyl."

Main Idea • 1. What is the passage mainly about?
- a. the renewed nostalgia for turntables
- b. trendy hipsters, Baby Boomers, or Generation Xers
- c. the growing trend of listening to and collecting vinyl records
- d. the streaming and collecting of digital music

Detail • 2. Which of the following has contributed to the increased popularity of vinyl records?
- a. turntables
- b. VR glasses
- c. pieces of art
- d. the Baby Boomers

Detail • 3. Which of the following is NOT missed by people who feel nostalgic about vinyl?
- a. the clean and polished sound
- b. the artwork on record sleeves
- c. the time spent in music shops
- d. lowering the needle onto a record

Detail • 4. Which of the following is NOT true about vinyl record collectors?
- a. They want to own a part of the musicians they admire.
- b. Price does not matter to them.
- c. Many play their records on turntables.
- d. They own records as pieces of art.

Detail • 5. What do Arctic Monkeys, the Strokes, and the White Stripes prefer?
- a. analog sound
- b. ultra-clean digital sound
- c. indie bands
- d. playing music on turntables

Vocabulary • 6. Which of the following words does NOT describe analog sound?
- a. warm
- b. rich
- c. deep
- d. clean

Inference • 7. What can be inferred about music from the phrase "technology has been taking us in the wrong direction" in the last paragraph?
- a. Technology has not created higher quantities and speeds.
- b. Technology has not led to higher sound quality.
- c. Technology has not created higher-quality turntables.
- d. Technology has led to better sound quality.

Summarizing Information

A. Read the passage again. Then, complete the outline below. Use the words in the box.

admire	sleeves	fed up	comeback
vinyl records	crave	pristine	nostalgic

Vinyl records are making a ¹_____ thanks to hipsters, Baby Boomers, Generation Xers, and others who feel ²_____ about the turntable.

People Feeling Nostalgic	Vinyl Collectors	Analog Sound Lovers
a. Miss the experience of owning ³_____ b. Miss looking at artwork on record ⁴_____	a. Want to have a part of the musicians they ⁵_____ b. Preserve their records in ⁶_____ condition	a. Are ⁷_____ with the digital music sound b. ⁸_____ the warm, rich analog sound

B. Complete the summary below with your own words.

People who feel nostalgic about ❶_____ are bringing vinyl records back into fashion. These people include hipsters, Baby Boomers, and ❷_____.

These people miss the ❸_____ of buying and owning vinyl records.

Others want to own ❹_____ of the musicians they love and admire.

And then there are those who simply must have the ❺_____ analog sound.

Even music bands such as ❻_____, the Strokes, and the White Stripes prefer the analog sound. They have been ❼_____ solely on vinyl records.

As a matter of fact, people ❽_____ are returning to vinyl. This is a reminder that technology ❾_____ better quality. When it comes to sound, analog is still ❿_____ digital.

Vocabulary in Context

A. The box below has words/phrases from the passage. Use them to complete the following sentences.

| hipsters | crave | flip through | solely | blame | abandoned |

1. My brother likes to _____ the racks of clothes on sale.

2. She is _____ interested in collecting antique toys, not new ones.

3. Many _____ hang out in Brooklyn's popular bars and restaurants.

4. I always _____ ice cream when I pass by Mindy's Ice Cream Store.

5. Animal protection organizations are worried about the high number of _____ animals.

6. I _____ the cloudy weather for my gloomy mood.

B. Choose the correct words/phrases from the passage to complete the sentences below.

1. I couldn't help _____ the chef's skillful work on that delicious ice cream cake.

   a. admiring   b. craving

2. The color purple is making a _____ with hipsters.

   a. boom   b. comeback

3. The _____ of the album are decorated with original artwork.

   a. sleeves   b. tracks

C. Determine the connotation (positive or negative meaning) of the underlined words.

	Positive	Negative
1. Some teachers insist on maintaining <u>analog</u> teaching methods in an increasingly digital learning environment.	☐	☐
2. The <u>boom</u> in American shale oil fields is increasing pollution around the world.	☐	☐

D. Use the following adjectives from the passage to write sentences in the box below.

Adjectives	Your Sentence
1. fed up (= tired of something)	*Who isn't **fed up** with all the new regulations?*
2. pristine (= clean as new)	
3. nostalgic (= feeling sentimental about the past)	
4. favorite (= most loved)	

Reading Connections

Read the following fun facts about vinyl records. Then, do the exercises.

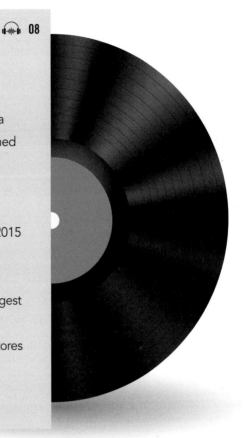

Fun Facts
About Vinyl

🎧 08

- The first vinyl record was released in 1931. It was a recording of Beethoven's *Fifth Symphony* performed by the Philadelphia Symphony Orchestra.
- The best-selling vinyl record of all time is Michael Jackson's *Thriller*. It sold 66 million copies.
- The most expensive vinyl record ever sold is the 2015 album *Once Upon a Time in Shaolin* by Wu-Tang Clan. It sold for 2 million dollars.
- Brazilian billionaire Zero Freitas has the world's largest vinyl record collection: over 6 million records and growing. He buys out the entire stock of record stores when they go out of business. He buys from the United States, Europe, and South America.

Comprehension Check
Check (✓) *True* or *False* for each of the following sentences.

	True	False
1. The first vinyl record was *Thriller*, which was released in 1931.	☐	☐
2. Beethoven's *Fifth Symphony* album sold 66 million copies.	☐	☐
3. *Once Upon a Time in Shaolin* was sold for 2 million dollars.	☐	☐
4. Zero Freitas owns over 6 million albums.	☐	☐
5. Freitas owns records stores in the U.S., Europe, and South America.	☐	☐

Reflections The return to vinyl is not the only return to the analog world of the past. Some people are now using mechanical typewriters for an analog feel while others are restoring and driving old cars that lack computers or digital components. Will the return to analog continue in the future, or is it just a passing trend?

3

Self-Improvement Ⓐ

Debug
Your Life

Unit Preview

A. Discuss the following questions.

1. Can you think of a difficult problem you faced in your life? How did you solve it?

2. What is the most urgent problem that you need to solve at the moment? Have you found an answer for it?

B. Match the words with the definitions below. Discuss your answers.

1. _____ in high demand (*phr.*)   a. greatly desired or sought after

2. _____ critical (*adj.*)   b. to find something by chance

3. _____ tackle (*v.*)   c. essential; vital

4. _____ stumble upon (*phr.*)   d. a problem that is a part of a larger problem

5. _____ colossal (*adj.*)   e. unable to find an answer or solution

6. _____ stuck (*adj.*)   f. to deal with; to address

7. _____ sub-problem (*n.*)   g. to stop doing something to reconsider it

8. _____ take a step back (*phr.*)   h. a method; a strategy

9. _____ perspective (*n.*)   i. huge; gigantic

10. _____ approach (*n.*)   j. a point of view; an outlook

C. Read the statements and check (✓) *Agree* or *Disagree*. Check the statements again after reading the passage to see whether your opinion has changed.

Statement	Before Reading		After Reading	
	Agree	Disagree	Agree	Disagree
1. You need great instincts to solve tough problems.				
2. Problems cannot be solved until you clearly understand them.				
3. If you cannot find an answer to a problem, it is best to ask someone else for help.				

Q1

What skills are necessary to solve problems in life?

Life is full of problems, big and small. Solving them takes commitment, creativity, emotional intelligence, and the abilities to conduct research, to analyze information, and to make decisions. Good problem-solvers are in high demand in all professions.

Unsolved problems can cause daily stress.

But what if you are not very good at solving problems? Is there a way to improve this critical skill and to tackle problems at work and in life with more confidence?

Q2

Is the random selection of solutions an effective way to solve problems?

The answer is yes, and it is based on a practice that comes from computer programming: debugging. To debug a computer program means to find and fix its errors, known as bugs. But what is the best way to debug a problem? Trying out solution after solution until you stumble upon the right one? Do you need luck to be a good debugger? The answer is no. Blindly trying out solutions is a colossal waste of time. You need a strategy.

The first step in this strategy is to understand the problem. You must know exactly what the problem is. Do you always understand the problems you are facing? If you can explain them in simple language, then you do. If you are stuck trying to explain them, then you do not. It is that simple. Renowned physicist Richard Feynman said this about understanding a problem: "If you can't explain something in simple terms, you don't understand it." Once you understand the problem, write it down. Make a diagram. Tell someone about it. It could go like this: "Jenny, can I tell you something? I can't get along with my mother."

You often need to break down a problem into smaller pieces.

25

The next step is to analyze the problem and to break it down into smaller problems. Do not try to solve the whole problem at once. Your problem has now become sub-problems A, B, and C. Begin with the simplest one (sub-problem A) and work your way up to the most difficult one (sub-problem C). For example, sub-problem A could become: "My mother and I never agree on anything."

30

The third step is to plan solutions for each sub-problem and then to solve them. If you get stuck on a sub-problem, do not get discouraged. Return to debugging; go step by step through your solution to figure out what went wrong. Or take a step back and look at the solution from another perspective. Research other ideas. Sometimes you may need to change the approach and start from the beginning. A solution to sub-problem A might be: "My mother and I need to discuss the reasons behind our opinions."

35

When you are done, connect the solutions to the sub-problems. That will give you the answer to the larger problem. And do not expect to become an expert problem-solver overnight. It takes lots of practice.

40

TIP

Summarize When You Get Confused

Reading can become confusing, especially when you start to lose focus. If that happens, stop reading. Now, without re-reading, summarize aloud or in your head what you have comprehended so far. Look back through the text and compare your summary with what is written on the page. Have you captured the important points? Do you understand the text better now that you have put it into your own words? Keep reading and repeat this process whenever the reading becomes confusing again. The more you summarize the reading in your own words, the better you will understand it. This will also help you remember in more detail the information you have just read.

Reading Comprehension

Main Idea **1. What is the passage mainly about?**
   a. developing your problem-solving skills through debugging
   b. improving your understanding of problems
   c. boosting your commitment, creativity, and emotional intelligence
   d. upgrading your ability to analyze problems

Detail **2. What is the meaning of debugging?**
   a. understanding errors
   b. searching for solutions to errors
   c. improving creativity to solve errors
   d. finding and fixing errors

Reference **3. What does <u>it</u> in paragraph 3 refer to?**
   a. strategy   b. problem   c. diagram   d. language

Detail **4. Which of the following is NOT true according to the passage?**
   a. You need luck to be a good debugger.
   b. If you can explain a problem in simple terms, then you understand it.
   c. You should solve the simplest sub-problem first.
   d. It takes time to become an expert problem-solver.

Vocabulary **5. Which of the following words is similar in meaning to blindly in paragraph 2?**
   a. creatively   b. randomly   c. intelligently   d. emotionally

Inference **6. What does paragraph 2 suggest about debugging?**
   a. It is a gigantic waste of time.
   b. It works best when a strategy is applied.
   c. It is a process of stumbling upon the right solution.
   d. It is a process of trying out strategy after strategy.

Inference **7. What can be implied from the passage?**
   a. Problem-solvers lack the confidence to tackle problems.
   b. A good debugger never gets stuck on a sub-problem.
   c. Maintaining a steady approach is important to solving problems.
   d. Everyone can improve their problem-solving skills.

Summarizing Information

A. Read the passage again. Then, complete the outline below. Use the words in the box.

approach   stuck   break it down
sub-problem   connect   debugging   terms

Problems in life can be solved by using a ¹_____ strategy. The strategy involves a step-by-step ²_____.

Step 1 Understand the problem you are facing; explain it in simple ³_____.

Step 2 Analyze the problem and ⁴_____ into simpler problems.

Step 3 Plan solutions for each ⁵_____. If you get ⁶_____, take a step back and rethink your solutions.

Step 4 ⁷_____ all your solutions to the sub-problems to solve the larger problem.

B. Complete the summary below with your own words.

Life's problems are solved through commitment, creativity, emotional intelligence, and the abilities to

❶_____, to analyze information, and to make decisions. People who possess these qualities are ❷_____ in all professions. For those who ❸_____, the practice of debugging can help them solve problems with more confidence. The debugging strategy should be conducted in a step-by-step approach. The first step in this strategy is to ❹_____ the problem you are facing. You should be able to ❺_____ in simple language. Next, you need to ❻_____ and to break it down into sub-problems.

❼_____ for each of these sub-problems. If you are having difficulties with a solution, debug it to figure out ❽_____. You may need to look at it ❾_____ or research other ideas. Finally, put together all your solutions to the sub-problems to arrive at the answer to

❿_____. Keep practicing this process to become a great problem-solver.

Vocabulary in Context

A. The box below has words/phrases from the passage. Use them to complete the following sentences.

| critical | tackle | colossal | commitment | figure out | intelligence |

1. I need to _____ a way to help my parents with the household expenses.

2. The project is _____ for our company, so I asked for help from all of the other departments.

3. Even though he is 30, he has the emotional _____ of an 18-year-old.

4. Today, my boss questioned my _____ to my work after I was 30 minutes late.

5. The Eiffel Tower is a _____ structure located in the heart of Paris.

6. The deadline is almost here, so we need to _____ the work with more enthusiasm.

B. Choose the correct words/phrases from the passage to complete the sentences below.

1. During the interview, Martha was questioned about her _____ in critical thinking.

   a. strategy   b. skill

2. I'm not sure I understand all the _____ written in my house rental contract.

   a. terms   b. problems

3. I guess I'm not a good _____; I've read this letter a hundred times, and I cannot find the spelling mistake that my boss said I made.

   a. debugger   b. planner

C. Determine the connotation (positive or negative meaning) of the underlined words.

	Positive	Negative
1. He stumbled through life without any direction until the day he won the lottery.	☐	☐
2. An unusually hot June was only the beginning of a long summer without rain.	☐	☐

D. Use the following phrases from the passage to write sentences in the box below.

Phrases	Your Sentence
1. in high demand (= greatly desired)	*Organic food is **in high demand** as people are becoming more health-conscious.*
2. take a step back (= to stop doing something in order to reconsider it)	
3. stumble upon (= to find something by chance)	
4. get stuck (= to be unable to make progress)	

Read the following tips for brainstorming solutions. Then, do the exercises.

🎧 10

Tips for Brainstorming Solutions

Problems need solutions. Good problem-solvers brainstorm solutions before coming up with a plan to solve a problem. The following are useful ways to brainstorm solutions.

1. Think of a few solutions. Do not settle for the first solution that comes to mind. Think of as many possible solutions as you can.
2. No solution is silly. Do not dismiss the ones that might seem extreme. Write them all down and be very specific when you word them.
3. Make sure that your solutions are not similar to each other.
4. Ask friends or colleagues for additional ideas. You never know where the answer to your problem may come from.

Comprehension Check
Check (✓) *True* or *False* for each of the following sentences.

	True	False
1. Brainstorming solutions is a key strategy for problem-solvers.	☐	☐
2. The first solution is the answer to any problem.	☐	☐
3. There is no such thing as a silly solution to a problem.	☐	☐
4. You should consider only solutions that are similar to each other.	☐	☐
5. When facing a problem, the worst thing you can do is ask for help.	☐	☐

Reflections   A bad solution to a problem is better than no solution at all. Do you agree or disagree with this statement? Why?

3

Self-Improvement B

Improve Focus Through *Zanshin*

Unit Preview

A. Discuss the following questions.

1. How do you avoid distractions while studying or working?

2. What is the latest goal that you have set for yourself?

B. Match the words with the definitions below. Discuss your answers.

1. _____	distraction (n.)	a. surprising; extraordinary
2. _____	circumstance (n.)	b. a diversion; interruption
3. _____	legendary (adj.)	c. to ignore or withstand an action or attraction
4. _____	bullseye (n.)	d. the center of a target in archery or shooting
5. _____	astounding (adj.)	e. a fact or condition that affects a situation
6. _____	feat (n.)	f. luxurious; fancy
7. _____	resist (v.)	g. an achievement; an accomplishment
8. _____	plush (adj.)	h. famous; renowned
9. _____	complacent (adj.)	i. routine; boring
10. _____	repetitive (adj.)	j. self-satisfied; content

C. Read the statements and check (✓) *Agree* or *Disagree*. Check the statements again after reading the passage to see whether your opinion has changed.

Statement	Before Reading		After Reading	
	Agree	Disagree	Agree	Disagree
1. The mind and body must be in harmony when doing a task.				
2. The loss of focus on a task can lead to bad results.				
3. Working toward a goal is more important than the goal itself.				

Q1

What is *zanshin*?

In Japanese, *zanshin* means "the mind with no remainder." The word is used mostly in the study of martial arts, and it describes the state of being aware of one's mind, body, and surroundings without any distractions. And with the minimum amount of effort. In other words, *zanshin* is the ability to maintain focus on a task under any circumstances.

According to Eugen Herrigel, a German professor who studied Japanese archery in the 1920s, legendary master archer Awa Kenzo was able to hit the bullseye every single time. And here is the truly astounding part: He was able to do it in complete darkness. This incredible feat was only possible through the application of *zanshin*.

For Kenzo, the end result—hitting the bullseye—was not important. What mattered most to him was the process: the body's position, the movement of the bow, the release of the arrow, and the breathing. Everything was done repeatedly to perfection. His mind and body were completely focused on the process without the distraction of thinking about the bullseye. When the process was perfect, the end result had to be perfect. For him, hitting the bullseye was the only possible outcome.

Q2

How can we apply *zanshin* to our lives?

The *zanshin* philosophy can be applied to every aspect of our lives. As long as we maintain complete awareness of the mind and body in relation to a goal, we have achieved *zanshin*. The key is to never lose our commitment to the process and to always resist distractions, especially the distraction of achieving a goal.

Say, for example, that you are a salesperson who has just exceeded the company's sales goals for the year. In fact, you were the top salesperson at the company, and as a reward, you were given a free vacation to Hawaii. You are now sitting in a plush beach resort sipping **sangrias**[1] and thinking about how wonderful your life is. You have become complacent; you are having fun. According to *zanshin*, you have just lost your focus and commitment because when you are relaxing, you are not improving.

In *zanshin*, idleness, having fun, and dreaming of results will distract you from the process of improving yourself. And in *zanshin*, process is everything. In order to successfully apply *zanshin* to our lives, we must fall in love with the process no matter how repetitive it may be. In a world where every salesperson dreams of free vacations, the one whose mind is empty and continues working and making sales is the only one improving. Like an archer shooting arrows in the dark, the target does not exist.

A woman focusing on her yoga posture

TIP

Keep a Logbook

Whenever you read a text, you should take the time to look up new and unfamiliar words or expressions. Enter these words and expressions in your logbook and review them regularly. When you look up the meaning of a word, also pay attention to its pronunciation and usage. Let's say you have just encountered the word "legendary," which is unfamiliar to you. This is how you would enter it in your logbook:

legendary (adjective) [ˈledʒənderi]
    1. relating to or characteristic of a legend
    2. well-known; famous
Example sentences:
    1. Ulysses is a **legendary** hero from Greek mythology.
    2. Michael Jordan is the most **legendary** basketball player of his time.

Through this entry, you can learn what part of speech the word "legendary" is (an adjective); how to pronounce it correctly (stress is on the first syllable, as shown by the stress mark ('); the different meanings of the word, depending on the context; and how to properly use the word in sentences. Write the example sentences yourself for better study practice. Do this for every new word and expression, and your vocabulary base and ability to use it properly will increase significantly.

---

1   **sangrias** Spanish mix drinks made of red wine, lemonade, fruit, and spices

Reading Comprehension

Main Idea • 1. What is the main idea of the passage?

    a. The outcome is more important than the process.

    b. A complacent mind is needed to continue improving.

    c. *Zanshin* can be used in every aspect of our lives.

    d. Japanese martial arts require complete awareness.

Detail • 2. Which of the following is considered a distraction to *zanshin*?

    a. maintaining focus on a task   b. being aware of one's body, mind, and environment

    c. thinking of the end result   d. staying committed to a task

Detail • 3. Which of the following is NOT true according to the passage?

    a. The end result was not important to Awa Kenzo.

    b. *Zanshin* is the ability to maintain focus in any circumstances.

    c. *Zanshin* means "the mind with no remainder" in Japanese.

    d. Eugen Herrigel was able to hit the bullseye every time.

Vocabulary • 4. Which of the following words has a similar meaning to idleness in the last paragraph?

    a. feat   b. relaxation   c. awareness   d. effort

Vocabulary • 5. Which of the following words has a different meaning from the others?

    a. goal   b. focus   c. end result   d. target

Inference • 6. What can be inferred from paragraph 5?

    a. Relaxing at the beach is a way of losing focus.

    b. Having fun increases one's commitment.

    c. Thinking positively about life can help one's focus.

    d. *Zanshin* is about achieving goals and winning rewards.

Inference • 7. What does the passage suggest about applying *zanshin* to our lives?

    a. It can help us improve ourselves if we love the process.

    b. It can help us improve ourselves if we become complacent.

    c. It can help us live more fun and relaxing lives.

    d. It can help us live lives without goals and rewards.

Summarizing Information

A. Read the passage again. Then, complete the outline below. Use the words in the box.

distract   awareness   end result
commitment   bullseye   process   martial arts

Paragraph 1: The word *zanshin* is used in the study of Japanese ¹＿＿＿＿＿＿＿＿＿. It refers to the ²＿＿＿＿＿＿＿＿＿ of one's mind, body, and surroundings without any distractions.

Paragraph 2: Through the use of *zanshin*, Awa Kenzo was able to hit the ³＿＿＿＿＿＿＿＿＿ every single time.

Paragraph 3: For Kenzo, the process was more important than the ⁴＿＿＿＿＿＿＿＿＿.

Paragraph 4: We can achieve *zanshin* in our lives by maintaining ⁵＿＿＿＿＿＿＿＿＿ to a process.

Paragraph 5: Having fun and thinking about goals can ⁶＿＿＿＿＿＿＿＿＿ our focus and commitment.

Paragraph 6: We must love the ⁷＿＿＿＿＿＿＿＿＿ if we hope to successfully apply *zanshin* to our lives.

B. Complete the summary below with your own words.

Zanshin, a Japanese word used in martial arts, describes the ability to ❶＿＿＿＿＿＿＿＿＿
on a task. *Zanshin* requires a state where one becomes aware of ❷＿＿＿＿＿＿＿＿＿,
and environment without any distractions. By practicing *zanshin*, ❸＿＿＿＿＿＿＿＿＿
Awa Kenzo was able to hit the bullseye even in complete darkness. To Kenzo, the process of shooting
an arrow ❹＿＿＿＿＿＿＿＿＿ than hitting the target. This process included the
❺＿＿＿＿＿＿＿＿＿, the movement of the bow, the release of the arrow, and the breathing.
We can achieve *zanshin* in our own lives by maintaining awareness of ❻＿＿＿＿＿＿＿＿＿
in relation to a goal. The key is to ❼＿＿＿＿＿＿＿＿＿ and to resist all distractions.
When we ❽＿＿＿＿＿＿＿＿＿, we lose our focus and commitment. To successfully apply
zanshin to our lives, we must ❾＿＿＿＿＿＿＿＿＿ the process. If our minds are empty,
❿＿＿＿＿＿＿＿＿.

Vocabulary in Context

| resist | circumstances | state | ability | feat | target |

1. The recent earthquake has made everyone live in a _____ of fear.

2. Because of his height, his greatest defensive _____ is to block shots around the basket.

3. I have to _____ the temptation of chocolate croissants if I hope to lose any weight.

4. Hiking to the top of this mountain is no easy _____.

5. I can't think of any _____ in which I would vote for this politician.

6. We used an empty bottle for a _____ and started throwing rocks at it.

B. Choose the correct words/phrases from the passage to complete the sentences below.

1. He was admonished many times by his dad for being _____.

    a. focused   b. complacent

2. This weekend, I'm only going to _____ and have some fun.

    a. relax   b. work

3. I hope we all learn from this defeat and _____ our performance in the next game.

    a. maintain   b. improve

C. Determine the connotation (positive or negative meaning) of the underlined words.

	Positive	Negative
1. His habit of <u>sipping sangrias</u> during work has been noticed by the boss.	☐	☐
2. The <u>repetitive</u> lifestyle of Buddhist monks focuses their minds on their beliefs.	☐	☐

D. Use the following adjectives from the passage to write sentences in the box below.

Adjectives	Your Sentence
1. legendary (= famous)	*The band's live performances have become **legendary**.*
2. astounding (= extraordinary)	
3. plush (= luxurious)	

Read the following description of mental awareness in Japanese martial arts. Then, do the exercises.

Four Minds to Victory in Japanese Martial Arts

🎧 12

In Japanese martial arts, everything begins and ends in the mind. There are many states of mind that must be mastered in any type of Japanese martial arts, be it karate, aikido, kendo, or others. The following four states of mind are essential to improve focus and preparedness in the arts of fighting:

1. **Shoshin** (beginner's mind). This state prepares one to learn without bias or judgment. *Shoshin* must be maintained as one advances through the levels of martial arts.
2. **Mushin** (no mind). This state refers to the empty mindedness of being fully focused on a task. In other words, there should be no distractions. *Mushin* can be achieved through meditation techniques.
3. **Fudoshin** (immovable mind). This state requires an unshakable determination. Nothing should stop one from achieving one's goal. One should have no doubts or hesitations.
4. **Zanshin** (the mind with no remainder). This state is an awareness of everything (mind, body, environment). This state must be maintained even after achieving a goal. It is a continuous process to perfect oneself.

Comprehension Check

Check (✓) *True* or *False* for each of the following sentences.

	True	False
1. The state of the mind is the most important thing in Japanese martial arts.	☐	☐
2. *Fudoshin* refers to a mind without bias and judgment.	☐	☐
3. *Shoshin* is the ability to learn without prejudice.	☐	☐
4. *Mushin* is all about the awareness of the self and the environment.	☐	☐
5. *Zanshin* must be continued even after reaching one's objective.	☐	☐

Reflections   *Zanshin* can take the fun out of life. Is this philosophy still relevant today, or is it something that was better suited for past eras?

The Santa Trackers

Unit Preview

A. Discuss the following questions.

1. Did you ever believe in Santa Claus? If so, at what age did you stop believing in Santa?

2. If you will have children, will you tell them Santa is real or just a Christmas story?

B. Match the words with the definitions below. Discuss your answers.

1. _____ agency (*n.*)   a. to form a mental image

2. _____ track (*v.*)   b. an organization

3. _____ sleigh (*n.*)   c. at the peak

4. _____ former (*adj.*)   d. a location

5. _____ whereabouts (*n.*)   e. in a harsh manner

6. _____ visualize (*v.*)   f. to follow; to keep an eye on

7. _____ lend a hand (*phr.*)   g. to help

8. _____ at the height (*phr.*)   h. in a nervous manner

9. _____ sternly (*adv.*)   i. previous

10. _____ anxiously (*adv.*)   j. a sled pulled by horses or reindeer

C. Read the statements and check (✓) *Agree* or *Disagree*. Check the statements again after reading the passage to see whether your opinion has changed.

Statement	Before Reading		After Reading	
	Agree	Disagree	Agree	Disagree
1. The Santa Claus spirit is getting stronger every year.				
2. Technology is making Santa Claus even more popular.				
3. Kids all over the world still believe in Santa Claus.				

The North American Aerospace Defense Command (NORAD) is the agency responsible for defending the United States against nuclear attacks. NORAD does its job 24 hours a day, 7 days a week, 364 days a year. One day each year, however, NORAD uses its network of satellites
5 and radars for a slightly different mission. That day is Christmas Eve. Its new mission? To track Santa Claus as he flies in his sleigh from the North Pole to the homes of children around the world.

Santa's flights have been tracked by NORAD since 1955. Thousands of volunteers have participated in this Christmas event through the years,
10 including former First Lady Michelle Obama. The volunteers answer emails and phone calls from children and let them know when Santa will be approaching their homes. And there are over 100,000 phone calls and 10,000 emails from children in about 200 countries to be answered.

In the past, NORAD used telephones, radio, TV, and newspapers
15 to report Santa's whereabouts. Today, it uses more high-tech media: Twitter, Facebook, an Internet website, the Amazon Alexa **AI virtual assistant**[1], and even an interactive computer game. NORAD also uses 3D maps with satellite imagery to visualize Santa's location. Other U.S. agencies, including NASA,

Q1
Why does NORAD track Santa's flight?

Google's Santa Tracker app on a Smartphone screen

have lent a hand to the Santa-tracking effort.

The story behind this yearly tradition has a bit of Christmas magic. It all started in 1955 with a phone call to the red phone—a special line that connected NORAD with U.S. military commanders. If it rang, it meant trouble. And in 1955, at the height of the Cold War between the Soviet Union and the U.S., trouble could have meant nuclear war. The man in charge at NORAD, Colonel Harry Shoup, picked up the phone and answered sternly, "Colonel Shoup!" On the other end of the line was the frightened voice of a little boy asking, "Is this Santa Claus?" It seems a Sears Department Store had advertised the wrong number for Santa's private phone in a newspaper ad. The number given was the secret red phone number. Colonel Shoup realized the mistake and answered, "Of course, this is Santa Claus."

Colonel Shoup then ordered his entire staff to answer Santa phone calls, which kept on coming that Christmas Eve in 1955. The Santa-tracking tradition has continued every year since 1955, and today, the Santa phone lines are busier than ever. On Christmas Eve, thousands of volunteers follow their nine-page Santa Tracker manuals to answer phone calls from children who are anxiously waiting for their gifts and for a visit from Santa.

Q2

How did the little boy get NORAD's secret phone number?

Santa riding in a sleigh loaded with gifts for children

TIP

Decode the Text

To decode text means to figure out the meanings of words or sentences in a reading passage. When you are trying to understand a new word, try to recognize parts of the word and think about how it could make sense in the text you are reading. Let's look at the example of "AI virtual assistant." This is a compound word formed by the word pairs "artificial intelligence" (AI) and "virtual assistant." You may know that "artificial intelligence" refers to a computer program. You may also know that "virtual" is related to the Internet or being online, as in "virtual reality"—not in the real world. An "assistant" is a helper." If we put all the words together, we can get the meaning "a computer helper" or even "an online computer assistant." If we then think of the context of the passage, we can deduce the meaning as "a computer program that helps us find an answer or do a task."

---

1   **AI virtual assistant** a computer program that understands voice commands and provides answers or completes given tasks. Examples are Apple's Siri, Amazon's Alexa, or Samsung's Bixby.

Reading Comprehension

Main Idea

1. **What is the passage mainly about?**
   a. Colonel Shoup's Christmas Eve story
   b. a little boy who phoned Santa Claus
   c. Christmas magic
   d. NORAD's Christmas tradition of tracking Santa Claus

Detail

2. **What is NORAD's job throughout the year?**
   a. to track Santa Claus as he flies over the U.S.
   b. to escort Santa Claus to the homes of children
   c. to defend the U.S. against nuclear attacks
   d. to answer the phone calls of children who want to talk to Santa Claus

Detail

3. **Which of the following is NOT true about the former First Lady mentioned in the passage?**
   a. Her name is Michelle Obama.
   b. She answered phone calls from children.
   c. She called the children to let them know about Santa Claus.
   d. She volunteered for the Santa-tracking event.

Detail

4. **What did the red phone connect NORAD with?**
   a. the Soviet Union   b. trouble
   c. U.S. military commanders   d. Colonel Harry Shoup

Vocabulary

5. **Which of the following words is unrelated to the others?**
   a. Facebook   b. website   c. newspapers   d. agency

Inference

6. **What does the passage suggest about the Santa-tracking tradition?**
   a. It has been conducted by NASA annually since 1955.
   b. It all started with a mistaken phone call from Colonel Shoup.
   c. It is possible due to the work of thousands of volunteers.
   d. It is now less popular than ever.

Inference

7. **What can be inferred from the passage about NORAD?**
   a. It will let U.S. military commanders lead the Santa-tracking tradition.
   b. It switched to high-tech media to update its Santa-tracking methods.
   c. It shared its secret phone number with a Sears Department Store.
   d. It no longer focuses on defending the U.S. against nuclear attacks.

Summarizing Information

> volunteers   advertised   Colonel Shoup   nuclear attacks
> satellites   since 1955   Santa's location   find out

Paragraph 1: a. NORAD defends the U.S. against ¹_____.

             b. On Christmas Eve, NORAD uses its radars and ²_____ to track Santa Claus.

Paragraph 2: a. Children call NORAD to ³_____ Santa's whereabouts.

             b. The ⁴_____ for NORAD's Christmas event answer their phone calls and

               emails.

Paragraph 3: NORAD uses high-tech media such as 3D maps to visualize ⁵_____.

Paragraph 4: a. Sears had ⁶_____ the wrong phone number for Santa.

             b. ⁷_____ pretended to be Santa when he answered a small boy's phone call.

Paragraph 5: The tradition of tracking Santa has continued every year ⁸_____.

NORAD is the agency that protects the U.S. from ❶_____.

During ❷_____, NORAD has another job: to track Santa Claus. On that day,

NORAD uses its ❸_____ to track Santa's flight from the North Pole to the

❹_____ around the world. More than 100,000 calls and 10,000 emails from

children have been answered by volunteers such as ❺_____. The Santa-tracking

tradition started in 1955 with a phone call to NORAD from ❻_____. The boy got the

secret ❼_____ from a mistaken Sears advertisement. NORAD's Colonel Shoup

realized the mistake and pretended to be ❽_____. Ever since that day,

NORAD has continued the tradition of ❾_____ from children and tracking Santa.

Today, NORAD uses media such as Facebook, ❿_____, a website, and even a

computer game to let children know Santa's whereabouts.

Vocabulary in Context

A. The box below has words/phrases from the passage. Use them to complete the following sentences.

| former interactive at the height agency visualize imagery |

1. The _____ CEO of the company is now enjoying her retirement.

2. Their latest _____ online computer game has been a huge success.

3. I'm trying to _____ how our garden will look covered in snow.

4. The _____ in this painting reminds me of my last trip to Southern Europe.

5. We booked our hotel reservations through a travel _____.

6. _____ of its power, Rome was the greatest city on Earth.

B. Choose the correct words/phrases from the passage to complete the sentences below.

1. The old man asked the two teenagers to _____ with his shopping bags.

    a. lend a hand   b. volunteer

2. Since the robbery, the police have been very interested in Jimmy's _____.

    a. whereabouts   b. AI virtual assistant

3. NASA is the _____ responsible for space exploration.

    a. network   b. agency

C. Determine the connotation (positive or negative meaning) of the underlined words.

	Positive	Negative
1. Oppressive governments constantly <u>track</u> the movements and actions of people.	☐	☐
2. Rescue dogs are highly trained in their <u>mission</u> to save lives.	☐	☐

D. Use the following adverbs from the passage to write sentences in the box below.

Adverbs	Your Sentence
1. sternly (= in a harsh manner)	*The teacher spoke **sternly** to the misbehaving children.*
2. anxiously (= in a nervous manner)	
3. slightly (= to a small degree)	

Reading Connections

The process of tracking Santa Claus is very precise. NORAD uses a combination of radars, satellites, and planes to simulate and keep track of Santa's flight. The chart below outlines this virtual process. Read the following process chart. Then, do the exercises.

🎧 14

How NORAD Tracks Santa Claus

First, NORAD uses its 50 radar installations in northern Canada and Alaska (the North Warning System) to see when Santa leaves the North Pole in his flying-reindeer sleigh.

NORAD then uses its system of satellites to track Santa's route. The satellites are 22,000 miles above Earth and use infrared sensors to detect the heat from Rudolph's red nose.

Next, NORAD turns on its SantaCams, which are a series of cameras installed in different countries around the world. When Santa appears at these locations, NORAD downloads the images of Santa onto its NORADSanta.org. The whole world can see Santa at this time.

Santa does not fly alone. He is escorted by Canadian CF-18 fighter planes over Canadian skies, and then by American F-15, F-16, or F-22 fighter planes over American skies.

Comprehension Check

Check (✓) *True* or *False* for each of the following sentences.

	True	False
1. The North Warning System can see when Santa leaves the North Pole.	☐	☐
2. The SantaCams are installed 22,000 miles above Earth.	☐	☐
3. NORAD's satellites are located in northern Canada and Alaska.	☐	☐
4. NORAD downloads images of Santa on its website.	☐	☐
5. Santa is virtually escorted by American and Canadian fighter planes.	☐	☐

Reflections   NORAD's yearly Santa-tracking event can be fun for kids and it brings them hope. However, should the volunteer time and the money spent on this event be used for helping children in more realistic ways?

Limitless
3D Printing

Unit Preview

A. Discuss the following questions.

1. Do you know the difference between 2D printing and 3D printing? Explain it in a simple way.

2. What would be the first object you would print with a 3D printer?

B. Match the words with the definitions below. Discuss your answers.

1. _____ shape (*v.*)   a. slow; tedious

2. _____ consecutive (*adj.*)   b. the first model or example; a sample

3. _____ take shape (*phr.*)   c. to produce

4. _____ latest (*adj.*)   d. to give a particular shape or form

5. _____ get around something (*phr.*) e. infinite; without limit

6. _____ prototype (*n.*)   f. to develop into something familiar

7. _____ generate (*v.*)   g. following in a continuous sequence

8. _____ serving (*n.*)   h. to overcome a problem

9. _____ limitless (*adj.*)   i. most recent

10. _____ time-consuming (*adj.*)   j. a portion; an amount

C. Read the statements and check (✓) *Agree* or *Disagree*. Check the statements again after reading the passage to see whether your opinion has changed.

Statement	Before Reading		After Reading	
	Agree	Disagree	Agree	Disagree
1. We can create any objects at home with 3D printers.				
2. Manufacturing is moving to individual homes.				
3. 3D printers will become as common as smartphones.				

Q1

How does additive manufacturing (3D printing) work?

In traditional manufacturing, pieces are cut from larger blocks of materials such as wood, plastic, glass, or metals and then shaped into various products. The opposite of this process is called additive manufacturing, or 3D printing. In additive manufacturing, a 3D printer

5   adds consecutive layers of material until the final product takes shape. A computer system controls this process using software such as CAD (computer-aided design). The latest 3D printers can manufacture products from almost any material, including glass, metal, and even food.

Although humans have been manufacturing glass for thousands of

10 years, finding a way to print 3D glass objects had been nearly impossible. The reason is that making glass requires very hot temperatures of more than 1,000 degrees Celsius. The recent discovery of a new material, however, has enabled scientists to get around the heat problem. The material, called liquid glass, is made of tiny particles of silica measuring

15 only 40 nanometers. That is about 2,500 times thinner than human hair! Liquid glass can be printed in different colors, such as green, blue, and red. Moreover, the resulting glass is clear enough to be used in camera lenses.

Machines that can print metal products have been around for a while,

20 but the process was extremely slow and expensive. That all changed in 2017, when a company released

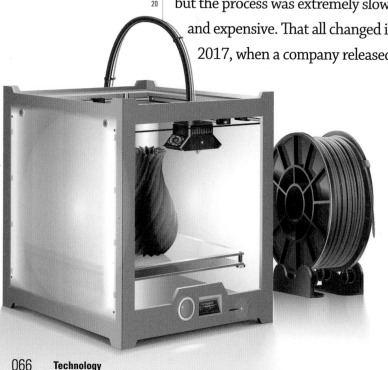

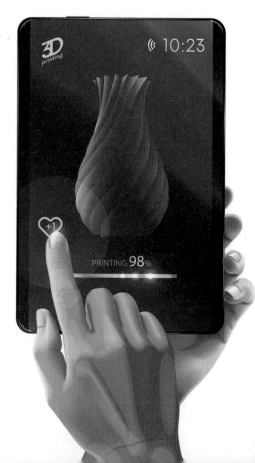

the first metal 3D printer costing less than $100,000. In the same year, another company developed a prototype machine that could print metal products 100 times faster than previous 3D printers. And the printing of metal has gotten much easier as companies are now selling software that generates designs ready for printing.

Food is another product that requires manufacturing. And like any other manufacturing process, making food is time consuming. This is not to mention the fact that the shape of the food is not easy to control. The solution to these problems is printed food. It is possible now to program a 3D food printer to print a hamburger in the shape of the Eiffel Tower, for example. Or it can make a serving of spaghetti in the shape of a lobster. This can all be done in very little time.

The 3D printing of a hamburger

Q2
What are the advantages of 3D printed food?

No doubt, the future of manufacturing belongs to 3D printing. Imagine a future where your computer is connected to a 3D printer. You just broke a wine glass from your favorite six-piece wine glass set? No problem. All you have to do is go online, download the design and feed it into your 3D printer, and in a few hours a new glass will be printed for you. It is as simple as that, and the possibilities are limitless.

TIP

Visualize the Reading

To visualize the reading means to form a picture in your mind of the things you are reading about. Strong readers always visualize the information they come across as they read. Visualizing will help you better understand the ideas or concepts you are reading. Take the example of additive manufacturing. This is perhaps a difficult concept because we are not familiar with seeing shapes being built in a gradual way. However, if we visualize a nozzle slowly adding layer upon layer of material in a 3D space inside a machine that looks like a box, then the process becomes clearer. Visualize something concrete, like a hand being printed in a white plastic material. Imagine the nozzle forming the wrist and then the rest of the hand all the way to the fingertips. When you visualize something, let your imagination create lots of detail. Try to use all your senses when you visualize. Would the plastic hand be smooth to the touch? Would it have a specific smell?

Reading Comprehension

Choose the best answers to the following questions on the passage "Limitless 3D Printing."

Main Idea

1. What is the main idea of the passage?
   a. Humans have been manufacturing for thousands of years.
   b. The possibilities for 3D printing are limitless.
   c. Additive manufacturing has replaced traditional manufacturing.
   d. The future belongs to materials such as glass, metal, and food.

Detail

2. Which of the following is NOT true about the 3D printing process?
   a. It is called additive manufacturing.
   b. It is based on traditional manufacturing.
   c. It is controlled by computer-aided design (CAD).
   d. It involves adding layers of material.

Detail

3. What is liquid glass made of?
   a. particles of silica   b. human hair
   c. camera lenses   d. colored glass

Detail

4. Which of the following is NOT true according to the passage?
   a. 3D metal printers costing less than 100,000 dollars are now available.
   b. Hamburgers can be 3D printed in the shape of the Eiffel Tower.
   c. The first metal printer was introduced in 2017.
   d. Temperatures of over 1,000 degrees Celsius are required to make glass.

Vocabulary

5. Which of the following words is unrelated to the others?
   a. prototype   b. food   c. glass   d. metal

Inference

6. What does the passage suggest about metal 3D printing?
   a. Previous 3D printers are much faster than prototype machines.
   b. Some people sell their own designs that are ready for printing.
   c. 3D printers are becoming more expensive.
   d. Available designs are making 3D printing much easier.

Inference

7. What can be inferred from the last paragraph about 3D printing in the future?
   a. Any object can be 3D printed in a matter of hours.
   b. The future of traditional manufacturing belongs to 3D printing.
   c. A limitless number of free designs will be available for 3D printing.
   d. We will be able to 3D print a glass full of our favorite wine.

Summarizing Information

A. Read the passage again. Then, complete the outline below. Use the words in the box.

quickly   additive   get around   liquid glass
spaghetti   manufacture   designs   silica

Today's 3D printers can ¹_____ products from glass, metal, and even food. The printers use a process called ²_____ manufacturing to shape these materials into objects.

Glass	Metal	Food
a. The 3D printing of glass was made possible by the discovery of ³_____. b. The material is made of ⁴_____ and can be printed in different colors.	a. The latest 3D metal printers can print objects very ⁵_____. b. Companies are selling software that can generate ⁶_____ ready for printing.	a. 3D food printers can ⁷_____ the problem of limited food shapes. b. A serving of ⁸_____ can be 3D printed in the shape of a lobster.

B. Complete the summary below with your own words.

❶_____, or 3D printing, is the process of adding consecutive layers of material until a final shape is achieved. A ❷_____ controls this printing process. Today's 3D printers can print from materials such as ❸_____. Colored glass can be printed from a new material called ❹_____. Metal 3D printing used to be ❺_____, but these days it has become much ❻_____. Making food is a ❼_____ manufacturing process. It is also not easy to control ❽_____. 3D printers can help by quickly ❾_____ in any desired shape. In the future, people will be able to 3D print anything they want. All they will have to do is ❿_____, feed it into the 3D printer, and wait for the object to be printed.

Vocabulary in Context

A. The box below has words/phrases from the passage. Use them to complete the following sentences.

particles	take shape	latest	generates	serving	time consuming

1. It's fascinating to watch glass _____ in the hands of these skilled artists.

2. Developing photographs from film was expensive and _____.

3. My brother loves eating; after he finishes his _____, he helps me finish mine.

4. The _____ trend is to wear clothes made of thinner, smarter materials.

5. The wind power plant _____ enough electricity for a small city.

6. Tiny _____ of sand can be carried by the wind for hundreds of kilometers.

B. Choose the correct words/phrases from the passage to complete the sentences below.

1. The chef finally completed a _____ of the spring menu.

   a. serving   b. prototype

2. At the manufacturing plant, workers _____ metal into frying pans.

   a. shape   b. generate

3. Nine _____ wins would be a new record for the team.

   a. limitless   b. consecutive

C. Determine the connotation (positive or negative meaning) of the underlined words.

	Positive	Negative
1. The robbers <u>got around</u> the security system by hacking it.	☐	☐
2. He never quits because his desire to win is <u>limitless</u>.	☐	☐

D. Use the following phrases from the passage to write sentences in the box below.

Phrases	Your Sentence
1. take shape (= to develop into something familiar)	*At the construction site, you can see the building slowly **take shape**.*
2. get around (= to overcome a problem)	
3. have been around (= have existed)	

Read about the following three types of 3D printing processes. Then, do the exercises.

🎧 16

There are several types of 3D printing processes, each suited for a particular type of material. The three printing processes described below are among the most commonly used ones.

The Three Most Common 3D Printing Processes

Fused Deposition Modelling	Stereolithography	Cartesian
This is the most popular printing process. Plastic is pushed through a hot nozzle (200 degrees Celsius). The nozzle moves around to print the required shape.	Printers using this process have a container of liquid plastic. A laser draws the object inside the liquid. As it is drawn, the object becomes solid until it reaches its final shape.	Cartesian 3D printers have X, Y, and Z axes and one or more motors that move along the axes to print the object on a square or rectangular base.

Comprehension Check
Check (✓) *True* or *False* for each of the following sentences.

	True	False
1. 3D printers are specialized for specific types of materials.	☐	☐
2. Fused deposition modelling is the least popular printing method.	☐	☐
3. Cartesian 3D printers have a container of liquid plastic.	☐	☐
4. Stereolithography 3D printers have a nozzle that moves around.	☐	☐
5. Printers using stereolithography have one or more motors.	☐	☐

Reflections   In the near future, 3D printers will become as common as refrigerators. Every home will have one. This will allow people to manufacture almost anything they can dream of in their homes. Manufacturing companies will gradually disappear. Will this coming manufacturing revolution improve our lives?

The Future of Hamburgers

Unit Preview

A. Discuss the following questions.

1. Do you like eating hamburgers? What is your favorite kind of hamburger?

2. Would you still eat hamburgers if they were made from meat grown in laboratories?

B. Match the words with the definitions below. Discuss your answers.

1. .... project (*v.*)   a. main; most important

2. .... looming (*adj.*)   b. cows

3. .... emission (*n.*)   c. to estimate

4. .... cattle (*n.*)   d. something unpleasant about to happen; imminent

5. .... initial (*adj.*)   e. the discharge of gases or radiation

6. .... patty (*n.*)   f. not expensive

7. .... edible (*adj.*)   g. existing or taking place at the beginning

8. .... affordable (*adj.*)   h. suitable or safe for eating

9. .... prime (*adj.*)   i. a round piece of meat to be cooked

10. .... vegetarian (*n.*)   j. a person who does not eat meat

C. Read the statements and check (✓) *Agree* or *Disagree*. Check the statements again after reading the passage to see whether your opinion has changed.

Statement	Before Reading		After Reading	
	Agree	Disagree	Agree	Disagree
1. People around the world need to change their eating habits.				
2. The beef of the future will be grown in labs.				
3. Fruit hamburgers can have a meaty taste.				

17

Q1

Why will the hamburger of the future need to change?

The meat hamburger has been and will continue to be a big part of our eating culture. But to meet humanity's future nutritional needs, the hamburger needs to change. The United Nations (UN) has projected that by 2050, the global population will be nearly 10 billion people. According

5   to the UN, the world's total food production needs to increase by 50 percent to provide enough food for 10 billion people. The answer to this looming problem is not meat.

Q2

What is the biggest problem with the present meat production?

Meat production can severely damage the environment. Currently about 3 percent of America's greenhouse gas emissions comes from

10   methane gas produced by cattle. Fast-food lovers need not worry though; the hamburger will still be on the menus of 2050. But hamburger meat will have to be replaced by meat alternatives such as lab-grown meats and meat-like fruits.

Scientists are already producing **synthetic meat**[1] in labs. And lab-produced meat seems to address all the worries related to the environment. According to a study published in the *Environmental Science and Technology Journal*, the production of synthetic meat requires up to 45 percent less energy. The process also reduces greenhouse gas emissions by up to 96 percent and makes use of only 1 percent of the land needed to produce regular meat.

For all its promise, the development of synthetic meat is in its initial stages. Scientists are trying to solve problems such as lowering production costs and giving the meat a more natural flavor. Production of a synthetic beef patty can cost as much as $300,000, and as for its taste, it can be barely edible. But scientists are predicting that affordable and tasty patties will be commercially available in a few years. One company is working on producing synthetic shrimp out of red algae, and NASA scientists have already created synthetic fish fillets. With all these alternatives, who needs meat?

But future hamburgers do not have to be synthetic. Nature has already provided us with an ideal alternative to beef: the jackfruit. This tropical fruit is extraordinary. It is the largest fruit in the world, and it is loaded with protein and nutrients such as vitamin B and potassium, and minerals such as iron and calcium. Most of all, it has the feel of meat, making it a prime alternative to replace beef. The jackfruit can be easily grown and therefore farmed. And who knows? It might just turn the meat lovers of today into the vegetarians of the future.

Pulled jackfruit burger

TIP

Discuss the Text with a Friend

If you feel confused about a text, it helps to discuss it with a friend. It is even better if your friend has not read the text yet. Explain it to your friend in your own words and also explain what confuses you. Sometimes we understand more than we think we do from a reading, and talking about the confusing part helps clear up misunderstandings. Software engineers call this method of explaining a problem "rubber duck debugging" because it is as if they explained a problem to a rubber duck. By saying the problem out loud, they can sometimes figure out the answer. Your discussion with a friend can have a similar effect. You will be surprised how much easier it is to understand a reading after you talk about it with a friend.

---

1   **synthetic meat** meat produced in labs by using stem cells to grow animal tissue

Reading Comprehension

Choose the best answers to the following questions on the passage "The Future of Hamburgers."

Main Idea • 1. What is the main idea of the passage?

    a. Future hamburgers will be grown in laboratories.

    b. Hamburgers will be replaced in the future by meat-like fruits.

    c. Future hamburgers will be made with synthetic and alternative meats.

    d. Hamburgers will disappear in the future.

Detail • 2. Which of the following is NOT mentioned as an advantage of synthetic meat production?

    a. It reduces greenhouse gas emissions.   b. It requires less energy.

    c. It uses far less land.   d. It increases animal welfare.

Detail • 3. Which of the following is a synthetic meat that has already been produced?

    a. the jackfruit   b. fish fillet

    c. shrimp   d. red algae

Detail • 4. Which of the following is NOT true about synthetic beef patties?

    a. Their production costs up to $300,000.   b. They taste great.

    c. They are not commercially available.   d. They will be affordable in the future.

Vocabulary • 5. Which of the following words has a different meaning from the others?

    a. artificial   b. alternative   c. synthetic   d. lab-produced

Inference • 6. What can be inferred from paragraph 1?

    a. Hamburgers need to have a different shape and taste in the future.

    b. The hamburger-eating culture needs to change in the future.

    c. Meat is the answer to humanity's future nutritional needs.

    d. The UN projects a small increase in humanity's 2050 nutritional needs.

Inference • 7. What does the last paragraph suggest about the jackfruit?

    a. It will turn all meat lovers into vegetarians.

    b. It contains the same nutrients and vitamins as beef.

    c. It has the same taste and feel as meat.

    d. It is a suitable replacement for beef.

Summarizing Information

A. Read the passage again. Then, complete the outline below. Use the words in the box.

synthetic   tasty   nutritional
environmental   culture   natural   farmed

Paragraph 1: a. The hamburger is an important part of our eating ¹_____.

b. Hamburgers need to change in order to meet humanity's future ²_____
needs.

Paragraph 2: Future hamburgers will be made with ³_____ meats and meat-like fruits.

Paragraph 3: Lab-produced meat can solve a lot of ⁴_____ problems.

Paragraph 4: Scientists are still working on affordable and ⁵_____ meat alternatives.

Paragraph 5: a. The jackfruit is a healthy and ⁶_____ alternative to meat.

b. Jackfruit can be easily ⁷_____.

B. Complete the summary below with your own words.

The world's population is projected to reach ❶_____ by 2050. This huge

population will need an additional 50% increase in the world's ❷_____.

The answer to this problem is not meat but ❸_____ and meat-like fruits.

Scientists are already producing ❹_____ in labs for the hamburgers of the future.

The production of synthetic meats can reduce ❺_____ and requires less energy

and land usage. For now, scientists are still working on lowering ❻_____

and giving meats ❼_____ In the near future, synthetic meats will be

❽_____ and tasty. But future hamburgers can also be made with

❾_____: the jackfruit. This healthy tropical fruit has the feel of meat and

is loaded with ❿_____, and protein.

Vocabulary in Context

cattle   project   emissions   patty   vegetarian   needs

1. The meat _____ in my cheeseburger had a dry and tough taste.

2. Public schools are not always meeting the educational _____ of our students.

3. CO_2 _____ are covering our cities in toxic clouds day after day.

4. A herd of _____ moved slowly toward the green grass next to the river.

5. She became a _____ and started practicing yoga at the age of 60.

6. Economists _____ a slow period of growth in the next few years.

B. Choose the correct words/phrases from the passage to complete the sentences below.

1. The jackfruit is a perfect example of a _____.

a. lab-grown fruit   b. meat-like fruit

2. Most nuts are an excellent source of minerals such as _____.

a. calcium   b. protein

3. Supporters of animal rights are against the sale of _____ furs.

a. synthetic   b. natural

C. Determine the connotation (positive or negative meaning) of the underlined words.

	Positive	Negative
1. Although its design looks great, the car is only in its <u>initial</u> stage of development.	☐	☐
2. This innovative recipe makes use of a variety of little-known <u>edible</u> plants.	☐	☐

D. Use the following adjectives from the passage to write sentences in the box below.

Adjectives	Your Sentence
1. ideal (= perfect; most suitable)	*In an **ideal** world, all people would have smiles on their faces.*
2. looming (= something unpleasant about to happen)	
3. affordable (= not expensive)	
4. prime (= main)	

Reading Connections

Read the following description of the jackfruit. Then, do the exercises.

 18

The Amazing Jackfruit

The jackfruit is an Asian tropical fruit. It grows in Thailand, Malaysia, India, Bangladesh, Nepal, Sri Lanka, the Philippines, and Brazil. It is the largest fruit in the world, and it can weigh from 3.5kg up to 25kg. The jackfruit has a sweet taste and pleasant smell. Even better, it has great medical benefits:

- The jackfruit contains vitamins C and A, thiamin, niacin, riboflavin, calcium, potassium, iron, zinc, sodium, and folic acid.
- It is rich in B-complex group vitamins as well as vitamin B6.
- It has anti-cancer, anti-hypertensive, anti-ulcer, and anti-inflammatory properties.
- It contains minerals, fiber, and protein and is free of saturated fats and bad cholesterol.
- It is antibacterial and antiviral, which is a great support to the immune system.
- It is low in calories. 100g of jackfruit only contains 94 calories.

Comprehension Check
Check (✓) *True* or *False* for each of the following sentences.

	True	False
1. The jackfruit grows in tropical countries around the world.	☐	☐
2. The jackfruit has a sour taste and a pleasant smell.	☐	☐
3. The jackfruit can weigh up to 25kg and is rich in vitamin B6.	☐	☐
4. The jackfruit is high in vitamins C and A and calories.	☐	☐
5. The jackfruit contains minerals, fiber, protein, and saturated fats.	☐	☐

Reflections   Even if meat from animals tastes better than laboratory-produced meat, should humanity switch to consuming artificial meat out of compassion for animals? Or are we justified in continuing to kill animals for our food needs?

Ghosts: The Science of Big Business

Unit Preview

A. Discuss the following questions.

1. Do you believe ghosts are real? Or do you believe they are imagined by people?

2. Have you ever seen or heard a ghost? If so, can you describe the event?

B. Match the words with the definitions below. Discuss your answers.

1. _____ spirit (*n.*)

2. _____ concrete (*adj.*)

3. _____ illusion (*n.*)

4. _____ stare back (*phr.*)

5. _____ conduct (*v.*)

6. _____ skull (*n.*)

7. _____ demonstrate (*v.*)

8. _____ cannot get enough of (*phr.*)

9. _____ profit (*v.*)

10. _____ rake in (*phr.*)

a. to show; to confirm

b. to earn a large amount of money

c. the bones that form the head

d. to carry out; to run

e. a false appearance or impression

f. to obtain a financial benefit

g. a ghost; the human soul

h. to constantly desire something

i. real; definite

j. to look back with interest

C. Read the statements and check (✓) *Agree* or *Disagree*. Check the statements again after reading the passage to see whether your opinion has changed.

Statement	Before Reading		After Reading	
	Agree	Disagree	Agree	Disagree
1. Many people throughout the world believe in ghosts.				
2. Science cannot prove the existence of ghosts.				
3. Businesses make a lot of money from ghost-related merchandise.				

19

A hotel in the U.S. known for being haunted

Q1

What have scientists been able to show regarding ghosts?

According to a 2013 Harris Poll, 43 percent of Americans believe in ghosts. The belief in ghosts—spirits that live in another dimension after death—is not unique to Americans. It is actually held in most societies around the world. Taiwan, for example, has a ghost month, and as many as 90% of Taiwanese have reported seeing ghosts. Yet despite so many people believing in and even seeing ghosts, science has not been able to provide any concrete evidence that ghosts exist.

Scientists have actually had more success showing how people's minds can create the illusion of ghosts. An Italian psychologist, for instance, had once looked at himself in a mirror and seen the face of an old man staring back at him. The psychologist later conducted a variety of experiments to determine the cause of this strange appearance. His experiments showed that under low light conditions, the brain tries to construct the image of a face not clearly visible by using any images, including faces of other people, skulls, and even faces of animals. Many other psychologists have demonstrated through experiments that ghosts are creations of the human mind.

While science cannot seem to find a single ghost, the world of business cannot get enough of them. There are TV shows, fiction and nonfiction books written on the subject, **ghost hunter**[1] organizations, merchandise sold during Halloween, ghost tours at "haunted" locations, and even electronic equipment built for the detection of ghosts.

Ghosts are big business, and even Hollywood is profiting. The six movies in the franchise *Paranormal Activity* have raked in close to $1 billion at the box office. Countless other movies about ghosts in the horror genre have brought Hollywood huge profits. Profits from ghosts are also made on Wall Street. After the market crash of 1929, many desperate businessmen jumped out of the buildings around Wall Street. Today, $25 ghost tours of the Wall Street area tell visitors that spirits are still walking around these streets.

Meanwhile, schools that teach the art of ghost hunting charge as much as $600 for a ghost hunter certification. And ghost hunters pay as much as $15,000 for electronic equipment that is needed to detect ghosts, such as motion sensors and infrared (IR) thermometers. But the biggest profits are made from Halloween merchandise sales, which top $5 billion in the U.S. alone. This is indeed a mega-business, with American consumers buying a large variety of Halloween items, from costumes to candy. The Halloween market has shown a steady rise since the early 2000s and is showing no signs of slowing down. Ghosts are big business and are here to stay.

People shopping for Halloween items

25

30

Q2
Which business profits the most from ghosts?

35

40

TIP

Build Up Your Reading Stamina

In order to improve your reading skills, you must understand your current reading limitations. Start by choosing passages from different texts that are unfamiliar to you (textbooks, essays, news articles, novels, etc.) and reading them in your normal style. As you read, notice when you begin to lose your reading stamina. If this happens after about 5-15 minutes, you should start building up your reading stamina. Next time, add one extra minute to your reading time and then take a break. Never continue reading past the moment you lose your reading stamina. Keep building it up one minute at a time.

---

1 **ghost hunter** an investigator of ghosts; a person who tries to tracks down ghosts

Reading Comprehension

Choose the best answers to the following questions on the passage "Ghosts: The Science of Big Business."

Main Idea

1. **What is the main idea of the passage?**
   a. The existence of ghosts has not been proven by science.
   b. Hollywood, Wall Street, and Halloween are big business.
   c. Ghosts may not be real, but they are big business.
   d. Many people believe ghosts are real and are here to stay.

Detail

2. **According to paragraph 2, what did the Italian psychologist see in the mirror?**
   a. the reflection of his own face
   b. the reflection of a ghost
   c. a real old man staring back at him
   d. an illusion created by his own mind

Detail

3. **How does the human brain try to construct the image of a face not clearly visible?**
   a. It uses low light conditions.
   b. It uses the faces of other people.
   c. It uses the experience of seeing ghosts.
   d. It uses psychological experiments.

Detail

4. **Which of the following is NOT mentioned in the passage?**
   a. A ghost hunter certification can cost as much as $600.
   b. About 10% of Taiwanese have not seen ghosts.
   c. Many Wall Street businessmen killed themselves in 1929.
   d. There are 25 types of Wall Street ghost tours available.

Vocabulary

5. **Which of the following words is unrelated to the others?**
   a. skull   b. ghost   c. spirit   d. appearance

Inference

6. **What does the last paragraph suggest about the Halloween market?**
   a. It is less profitable than the ghost-hunting business.
   b. It will continue to grow in the future.
   c. It sells many products, such as ghost detection equipment.
   d. It is restricted to American consumers.

Inference

7. **What can be inferred from the passage about ghosts?**
   a. Many people throughout the world have seen them.
   b. They exist in many parts of the world.
   c. They are created by the human mind.
   d. Big businesses believe they are real.

Summarizing Information

A. Read the passage again. Then, complete the outline below. Use the words in the box.

get enough of   demonstrated   evidence
hunters   reported   mega-business   profiting

Paragraph 1: a. As many as 90% of Taiwanese have ¹_____ seeing ghosts.

b. Science, however, has no clear ²_____ that ghosts exist.

Paragraph 2: Psychologists have ³_____ that ghosts are creations of the human mind.

Paragraph 3: The world of business cannot ⁴_____ ghosts.

Paragraph 4: Hollywood and Wall Street are ⁵_____ from ghosts.

Paragraph 5: a. Ghost ⁶_____ and related businesses are making money from ghosts.

b. Halloween merchandise is a ⁷_____, with sales over $5 billion in the U.S. alone.

B. Complete the summary below with your own words.

❶_____ is held by many people around the world. Despite this, science has not provided ❷_____ that ghosts exist. Instead, psychological experiments have shown that ghosts are created ❸_____. Experiments have demonstrated that the ❹_____ tries to construct ❺_____ not clearly visible by using the faces of other people, animals, and even skulls. In ❻_____, however, ghosts seem to be everywhere. Hollywood has ❼_____ from movies in the horror genre. Even Wall Street is profiting from ❽_____ where businessmen have jumped out of buildings. But the biggest profits are being made by sales of ❾_____. The Halloween market ❿_____ since the early 2000s and is showing no signs of a slowdown.

Vocabulary in Context

detect   spirits   construct   appearance   experiments   unique to

1. This rare language is _____ a small group of people.

2. More _____ are needed before the cancer medicine can be certified.

3. Police dogs can _____ drugs hidden in luggage.

4. Two kids are trying to _____ a car from Lego blocks.

5. The singer's _____ at the party surprised everyone.

6. It was believed that crows took away the _____ of dead people.

1. The story of Gandhi's life is an example of _____ writing.

   a. fiction   b. nonfiction

2. The fantasy _____ is a big money-maker for Hollywood these days.

   a. box office   b. genre

3. The office has _____ that turn the lights on when they detect movement.

   a. motion sensors   b. infrared thermometers

	Positive	Negative
1. Magicians create <u>illusions</u> to entertain their audiences.	☐	☐
2. The company has been recently accused of making war <u>profits</u>.	☐	☐

Phrases	Your Sentence
1. is big business (= is very profitable)	*Music streaming **is big business** for entertainment companies.*
2. stare back (= to look back with interest)	
3. cannot get enough (= to constantly desire something)	
4. rake in (= to earn a lot of money)	

Reading Connections

Read the following description of ghost-hunting equipment. Then, do the exercises.

🎧 20

Must-Have Ghost-Hunting Equipment

While ghosts have not been proven to exist, equipment for their detection is abundant. A modern-day ghost hunter is equipped with the latest electronic gadgets for finding elusive ghosts. The manufacturers of these gadgets are convinced that their products will work as advertised.

SLS Cameras	Electronic Voice Phenomena (EVP) Detectors	Paranormal Music Box (PMB) Radars
They can work in absolute darkness, detect spirits that cannot be seen with the naked eye, and display their locations on 3D maps. Price: Around $400	They can detect and record unexplained voices or sounds emitted by spirits. Price: Around $100	They can alert ghost hunters of a nearby ghost presence by playing music. Price: Around $400

Comprehension Check
Check (✓) True or False for each of the following sentences.

	True	False
1. Electronic equipment for finding ghosts is elusive.	☐	☐
2. Manufacturers of ghost-detection equipment believe in their products.	☐	☐
3. SLS cameras display the locations of spirits on 3D maps.	☐	☐
4. EVP detectors can create unexplained voices or sounds.	☐	☐
5. PMB radars can alert ghosts by playing music.	☐	☐

Reflections   If ghosts exist, why can't people see or hear them? Is it an ability that some people have and other people lack? Or does it require a more advanced sensory ability than eyes and ears, since cameras have not clearly captured ghosts either?

The Islands Surrounding Venice

Unit Preview

A. Discuss the following questions.

1. In what country is the city of Venice? What is Venice famous for?

2. Do you remember any movies that were set or filmed in Venice?

B. Match the words with the definitions below. Discuss your answers.

1. _____ canal (*n.*)   a. a photograph

2. _____ span (*v.*)   b. to take a picture

3. _____ crowd (*v.*)   c. a cure; a remedy

4. _____ stand out (*phr.*)   d. a protected nature area or park

5. _____ vibrant (*adj.*)   e. a natural or man-made waterway

6. _____ snap (*v.*)   f. to gather in a group

7. _____ snapshot (*n.*)   g. to attract attention

8. _____ antidote (*n.*)   h. to extend from one side to another

9. _____ preserve (*n.*)   i. bright; striking

10. _____ buff (*n.*)   j. a fan of something

C. Read the statements and check (✔) *Agree* or *Disagree*. Check the statements again after reading the passage to see whether your opinion has changed.

Statement	Before Reading		After Reading	
	Agree	Disagree	Agree	Disagree
1. Venice is an island surrounded by water canals.				
2. There are no forests or nature parks in Venice.				
3. You cannot ride a bicycle in Venice.				

21

Lacy white umbrellas, traditional souvenirs in Burano

The Italian city of Venice is actually built on 118 small islands that are separated by canals. Some 400 small bridges span the canals and connect the islands. The islands are part of the Venetian **Lagoon**[1], located on the Adriatic Sea. The local population numbers fewer than 300,000 people, but there are over 50,000 daily visitors who come to Venice to see its buildings and plazas. In the Old City Center there are no roads, so people travel around the canals by gondola or *vaporetto* (water bus).

The attractions in the Old City Center—the St. Mark's Square, the St. Mark's Basilica, and the Rialto Bridge—are known for their beauty all over the world. It is no wonder most tourists to Venice crowd around these attractions. But the crowds of people can be tiresome, and some people may prefer a quieter side of Venice. They have nothing to worry about. Venice has plenty of islands that can offer a more relaxed atmosphere. Among these, three stand out in beauty: Burano, Torcello, and Lido.

Q1

Where can you see a quieter side of Venice?

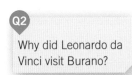

Q2

Why did Leonardo da Vinci visit Burano?

Burano is an island with colorful fairytale houses. The reason for their vibrant colors was quite practical: It allowed fishermen to find their homes after returning from a day at sea. Snap a picture if you find this setting romantic, as many visitors do. If romantic snapshots are not your thing, visit the Lace Museum to find out why Leonardo da Vinci purchased cloth here in 1481.

Colorful houses in Torcello

Torcello is mostly a natural park, the perfect antidote to a crowded Venice square. If you walk through the local forest preserve, your footsteps might follow the same path walked by Ernest Hemingway in 1948. Yes, the famous American writer spent some time here on Torcello. And if you are lucky, your footsteps will bring you to the Cathedral of Santa Maria Assunta. The cathedral was constructed in the 7th century and decorated with stunning Byzantine mosaics around the 11th century. You do not need to be a student of architecture to appreciate its beauty.

Finally, there is Lido. Movie buffs may have heard of this 11km-long island, since it hosts the annual Venice Film Festival. But even if you have never heard of Lido, you will have the perfect way to discover its charms: by rental bicycle. Lido is the only island in Venice where you can rent a bicycle and explore at your own leisurely pace. And why not? The air there is so fresh and the sunlight so soothing that you will not ever want to leave.

TIP

The Importance of Repeated Words

Important words (keywords) in a reading passage are often repeated. The repetition of words can emphasize and rein-force the importance of an idea or draw attention to details. In the passage "The Islands Surrounding Venice," the word **island(s)** is repeated several times, including in the title. This emphasizes the most important characteristic of Venice: that it is composed of islands. But islands, by their very nature, are also isolated places. This natural isolation points to the fact that islands can also provide relaxation and a break from busy city life. The more distant islands that surround Venice are quieter and more relaxing than the Old City Center. The ideas of isolation and relaxation are inherent in the word "island." It is always a good idea to ask yourself why a certain word is repeated in a reading passage. The answer might lead you to a better understanding of the text.

---

1   **lagoon** an enclosed, shallow body of salt water similar to a lake. Lagoons are separated from a sea or ocean by barrier islands, reefs, or man-made barriers.

Reading Comprehension

Main Idea • **1. What is the passage mainly about?**

    a. Venice's Old City Center and its main attractions

    b. the relaxing and peaceful islands around Venice

    c. Venice's 118 islands, 400 bridges, and canals

    d. a trip through Venice by gondola and *vaporetto*

Detail • **2. What made Burano's colorful houses practical in the past?**

    a. They attracted photographers to Burano.

    b. They created a romantic setting for tourists.

    c. They made fishermen feel like they lived in a fairytale.

    d. They allowed fishermen to find their way back home.

Detail • **3. Where can you can follow in Ernest Hemingway's footsteps through Torcello?**

    a. at the Venice Film Festival   b. at the Lace Museum

    c. through the forest preserve   d. through the St. Mark's Square

Detail • **4. Which of the following is NOT true according to the passage?**

    a. The population of Venice is over 300,000. b. Leonardo da Vinci visited Burano in 1481.

    c. Lido Island is 11km long.   d. Rialto Bridge is in the Old City Center.

Vocabulary • **5. Which of the following words is opposite in meaning to relaxed in paragraph 2?**

    a. quieter   b. leisurely   c. tiresome   d. soothing

Inference • **6. What does paragraph 4 suggest about the Cathedral of Santa Maria Assunta?**

    a. Its beauty can be appreciated by any student of architecture.

    b. Its beauty can be appreciated by anyone.

    c. Its beauty was only appreciated by Ernest Hemingway.

    d. Its beauty can be appreciated by any local resident.

Inference • **7. What can be implied from the passage?**

    a. Most tourists to Venice visit its surrounding islands.

    b. Most tourists to Venice visit the Old City Center.

    c. The number of daily visitors to Venice is greater than the local population.

    d. Tourists to Venice will not ever want to leave.

Summarizing Information

A. Read the passage again. Then, complete the outline below. Use the words in the box.

forest preserve   surround   soothing sunlight
Byzantine mosaics   fairytale   hosts   romantic snapshots

Burano, Torcello, and Lido are three beautiful islands that [1].. Venice.

Burano	Torcello	Lido
a. It has [2]................................ houses.	a. Its cathedral is decorated with [4].................................	a. It [6]................................ the annual Venice Film Festival.
b. It is a great location for [3].................................	b. It has a local [5].................................	b. It has fresh air and [7].................................

B. Complete the summary below with your own words.

The Italian city of Venice is a city located in the Venetian Lagoon on the waters of the ❶..
More specifically, it is built on ❷.. that are connected by 400 bridges. Traveling around
Venice is only possible by boat or ❸... The Venice Old City Center is crowded by
❹... They come here to see sites such as the ❺..
or the Rialto Bridge. The islands of Burano, Torcello, and Lido provide a more ❻...
There are many attractions on these islands, including Burano's ❼.. houses, Torcello's
7th century cathedral, and Lido's ❽... Famous people in history have visited
these islands; ❾.. bought cloth in Burano, and Ernest Hemingway walked through
the ❿.. of Torcello.

Vocabulary in Context

A. The box below has words/phrases from the passage. Use them to complete the following sentences.

| canal | stand out | vibrant | fairytale | preserve | tiresome |

1. Two images _____ in my mind: the sunrise and the sunset.
2. Hearing the same song played on every radio station can become _____.
3. Yellowstone National Park is a famous American nature _____.
4. Monet used a range of _____ colors in his paintings.
5. His idea of a _____ vacation is a week of sightseeing in Paris.
6. Two boats are slowly making their way up the _____.

B. Choose the correct words/phrases from the passage to complete the sentences below.

1. On the nightstand table was an old _____ of his grandparents.
   a. setting   b. snapshot
2. A large number of movie _____ travel to Hollywood in the hope of meeting their favorite stars.
   a. visitors   b. buffs
3. Every morning, people of all ages _____ the hiking trail to the Buddhist temple.
   a. crowd   b. stand out

C. Determine the connotation (positive or negative meaning) of the underlined words.

		Positive	Negative
1.	"This is not photography," said the art critic. "It has the look of a cellphone <u>snapshot</u>."	☐	☐
2.	The bad smell of the canal water in the summer is the <u>antidote</u> for romance.	☐	☐

D. Use the following verbs / phrasal verbs from the passage to write sentences in the box below.

Verbs / Phrasal Verbs	Your Sentence
1. stand out (= to attract attention)	*A 100-story skyscraper **stands out** among all the other buildings.*
2. crowd (= to gather in a group)	
3. span (= to extend between two sides)	
4. snap (= to take a picture)	

Reading Connections

Read the following hotel booking email. Then, do the exercises.

 22

New Message	_ ⤢ ×
To	reservations@villalinahotel.com Cc Bcc
From	janicewoodward@fabmail.com
Subject	**Booking request**

Dear Hotel Manager,

I would like to reserve accommodations for a suite at the Villa Lina Hotel for 3 guests for 5 days and 4 nights. The guests are Janice Woodward (me), Jeff Woodward (my husband), and Julie Woodward (my daughter). Julie is 7 years old.

We'll arrive on Burano on Monday, July 1, at approximately 11 a.m. We will be arriving by *vaporetto* from Torcello. Our departure date will be on Friday, July 5, at noon, when we will depart for Lido.

Please make sure that our booking includes a daily breakfast for 3 people. We also require a room with an Internet connection. If possible, the room should be located away from the elevator or any noisy facilities such as conference rooms.

Thank you for your attention to this matter. I look forward to your confirmation of the booking.

Kind Regards,
Janice Woodward

Send

Comprehension Check
Check (✓) *True* or *False* for each of the following sentences.

	True	False
1. Janice wants to make a booking for four people, including herself.	☐	☐
2. Janice and her family will arrive by gondola from Torcello.	☐	☐
3. Janice plans to spend four nights and five days on Burano.	☐	☐
4. Janice's next destination after Burano is Lido Island.	☐	☐
5. Janice asked for a room close to the elevator.	☐	☐

Reflections   The citizens of Venice see their city invaded by tens of thousands of tourists each day, causing them many inconveniences. Should Venice restrict the number of arriving tourists?

The Land at the World's End

Unit Preview

A. Discuss the following questions.

1. Who discovered Australia? Was it the British or the Dutch? Who colonized Australia?

2. Is Australia a tropical country, or does it have four seasons?

B. Match the words with the definitions below. Discuss your answers.

1. _____ sight (*v.*)　　　　　　a. located farthest to the south

2. _____ southernmost (*adj.*)　　b. a person who settles in a new area

3. _____ inhabited (*adj.*)　　　　c. extremely tall

4. _____ settler (*n.*)　　　　　　d. a large quantity of something

5. _____ notorious (*adj.*)　　　　e. to send people to a country to take control of it

6. _____ trace (*n.*)　　　　　　　f. a mark of a previous existence

7. _____ abundance (*n.*)　　　　g. occupied or populated by people

8. _____ towering (*adj.*)　　　　h. famous for a bad quality or deed

9. _____ climate (*n.*)　　　　　　i. to see; to observe

10. _____ colonize (*v.*)　　　　　j. the weather conditions in an area

C. Read the statements and check (✓) *Agree* or *Disagree*. Check the statements again after reading the passage to see whether your opinion has changed.

Statement	Before Reading		After Reading	
	Agree	Disagree	Agree	Disagree
1. The British are the original people of Australia.				
2. Prisons can be interesting places to visit.				
3. Australia has strikingly beautiful islands.				

23

The Australian continent was discovered by Dutch explorers, who named it "New Holland," in the 1600s. Today, Australia is divided into seven states, and the smallest of these states is an island called Tasmania. Tasmania itself is named after Dutch explorer Abel Janszoon Tasman, who first sighted it in 1642. The island is located 240km south of Australia, and it is closer to Antarctica than it is to Australia. Tasmania is one of the southernmost inhabited places on Earth.

The British colonized Australia in 1788 and arrived in Tasmania in 1803. Before the British arrival in Tasmania, the island, like the rest of Australia, had been inhabited by **aboriginals**[1] for thousands of years. In addition to free settlers, Britain also sent convicts to Australia and Tasmania. One of Tasmania's most notorious British colonial prisons was Port Arthur. The convicts held in these 18th-century prison buildings endured hard labor, torture, and extremely unhealthy living conditions. Nightly ghost tours are available here for tourists who feel brave enough to see these infamous, horror-filled buildings after sunset.

Aside from its many traces of history, Tasmania is also known as an excellent adventure travel destination. Tassie, as Tasmania is known to Australians, has an abundance of natural wonders. The island has every geographical feature: towering

Q1
Who were some of the early settlers in Tasmania? Where did they come from?

A view of the Port Arthur prison buildings

mountains, fast-moving rivers, green rainforests, white-sand beaches, and a unique wildlife. To see it, a variety of wildlife tours, from deep-sea fishing tours to rainforest trekking, are available. For adventure seekers, there are whitewater kayak courses on the Franklin River and guided tours through local forests. And there are plenty of hiking trails, from beginner courses to expert ones.

A wooden pier and clear water in Tasmania

The seasons in Australia are opposite the <u>ones</u> in northern countries. In Tasmania, summer is from December to February, and it is the peak of the tourist season. Autumn lasts until May. This is the time to see the beautiful color changes in the trees. Winter is from June to August, and yes, it does snow in Tasmania. Spring follows in September, giving Tasmania a four-season climate.

Q2
What type of climate does Tasmania have? When is it spring in Tasmania?

Travelers from all over the world also come to Tasmania for its music festivals. The 10-day Mofo Music Festival is a yearly display of some of the best music from around the world. Mofo is held in summer in January, but it has a sister music festival held here in the winter, called Dark Mofo. There are also food festivals, yacht races, and plenty of other ways to have fun in the land at the world's end. Just make the long trip down there!

TIP

The Importance of Synonyms

Important words (keywords) in reading passages are sometimes repeated through synonyms (similar words). Just like repeated words, synonyms can emphasize and reinforce the importance of an idea or draw attention to details. In the passage "The Land at the World's End," we can find synonyms and also similar expressions. The adjectives "notorious" and "infamous," for example, are used in the description of Port Arthur's prison buildings. These synonyms emphasize the fact that Tasmania's past is characterized by violence and cruelty. Meanwhile, the expressions "the land at the world's end" and "one of the southernmost inhabited places" are similar in meaning, showing that Tasmania's extreme location is one of its important features.

---

1   **aboriginals** the indigenous (native) people of Australia

Reading Comprehension

Main Idea

1. **What is the main idea of the passage?**
   a. Tasmania has a great climate for adventure travel.
   b. Tasmania was inhabited by aboriginals and colonized by settlers.
   c. Tasmania has plenty of historical and adventure tours, as well as entertaining events.
   d. Tasmania is one of the southernmost inhabited places on Earth.

Detail

2. **Which of the following is NOT available in Tasmania?**
   a. deep–sea fishing tours   b. movie festival guided tours
   c. rainforest trekking   d. whitewater kayak courses

Detail

3. **What do Australians refer to Tasmania as?**
   a. "the land at the world's end"   b. New Holland
   c. Tassie   d. Aussie

Reference

4. **What does the word <u>ones</u> in paragraph 4 refer to?**
   a. countries   b. people
   c. seasons   d. climates

Vocabulary

5. **Which of the following words is closest in meaning to the word display in the last paragraph?**
   a. trip   b. music   c. show   d. fun

Inference

6. **What does paragraph 2 suggest about the Port Arthur prison buildings?**
   a. They were inhabited by aboriginals.
   b. They were inhabited by settlers.
   c. They are closed to the public.
   d. They are scary places to visit.

Inference

7. **What can be inferred from the passage about Tasmania?**
   a. It has a convenient location for international tourism.
   b. Its climate is similar to Antarctica's climate.
   c. Its population is made up mostly of aboriginals and Dutch settlers.
   d. It is Australia's southernmost inhabited state.

Summarizing Information

yearly   wildlife   colonial   sister
hiking trails   destination   ghost   southernmost

Tasmania is one of the ¹_____ inhabited places in the world. Tasmania has something for everyone, from historical sightseeing to ²_____ adventure tours to entertaining music festivals.

History	Adventure	Entertainment
a. Port Arthur's ³_____ prisons were built by the British.	a. Tasmania is a top ⁵_____ for adventure travel.	a. The Mofo Music Festival takes place ⁷_____.
b. ⁴_____ tours are held at Port Arthur after sunset.	b. ⁶_____ range from beginning to expert levels.	b. Mofo's ⁸_____ festival is called Dark Mofo.

B. Complete the summary below with your own words.

The Australian continent is divided into seven states, and one of these states ❶_____ called Tasmania. Tassie, as Australians call Tasmania, is located ❷_____, very close to Antarctica. Australia and Tasmania ❸_____ by the British in the 18th century. Settlers were sent to these faraway lands, but the British also built prisons there and ❹_____ to these prisons. Port Arthur is a former 18th-century ❺_____ located in Tasmania. Today, Tasmania is known as a great destination for ❻_____. The mountains, rainforests, ❼_____ of Tasmania are unique in their beauty. Tourists to Tasmania are also attracted by the ❽_____. The ❾_____ are the most famous music festivals held in Tasmania. Tasmania's climate has four seasons: spring, summer, fall, and winter. The seasons in Tasmania, however, are opposite the seasons in the ❿_____. Winter, for example, is from June to August.

Vocabulary in Context

A. The box below has words/phrases from the passage. Use them to complete the following sentences.

sighted   inhabited   nightly   trace   colonized   towering

1. I can't find a single ⎯⎯⎯⎯⎯⎯⎯⎯ of food in your empty refrigerator.

2. K2 is a ⎯⎯⎯⎯⎯⎯⎯⎯ mountain peak in the Himalayan range.

3. Rome has been ⎯⎯⎯⎯⎯⎯⎯⎯ for about 28 centuries.

4. The tour company is offering ⎯⎯⎯⎯⎯⎯⎯⎯ riverboat tours of Bangkok.

5. The first thing we ⎯⎯⎯⎯⎯⎯⎯⎯ in the hotel lobby was a beautiful chandelier.

6. The French ⎯⎯⎯⎯⎯⎯⎯⎯ more than 20 African countries.

B. Choose the correct words/phrases from the passage to complete the sentences below.

1. Australian ⎯⎯⎯⎯⎯⎯⎯⎯ believed in spirits of nature such as mountain spirits.

    a. aboriginals   b. settlers

2. ⎯⎯⎯⎯⎯⎯⎯⎯ is often used as a means of obtaining information and confessions.

    a. hard labor   b. torture

3. You like sweets, and I hate sugar. In fact, most of our tastes in food are ⎯⎯⎯⎯⎯⎯⎯⎯.

    a. similar   b. opposite

C. Determine the connotation (positive or negative meaning) of the underlined words.

	Positive	Negative
1. Many hitters were scared of Nolan Ryan's <u>notorious</u> fastballs of over 100mph.	☐	☐
2. An <u>abundance</u> of cheap toys have flooded the market in the last year.	☐	☐

D. Use the following compound nouns from the passage to write sentences in the box below.

Compound Nouns	Your Sentence
1. natural wonder (= beautiful nature)	*The Amazon River is a **natural wonder** of Brazil.*
2. adventure seeker (= a person who enjoys adventures)	
3. wildlife tour (= a trip for viewing nature)	
4. hiking trail (= a path used for hiking)	

Read the following information on Port Arthur and its ghost tour. Then, do the exercises.

🎧 24

More than 1,000 people died at Port Arthur during the 47 years it was used as a prison by the British. Some people believe that many of the souls of the dead have never left Port Arthur. These ghost stories have been around Port Arthur since 1870. Today, the Port Arthur Historic Site offers a 90-minute lantern-lit ghost tour. A tour guide accompanies visitors through the site's infamous buildings and ruins and tells stories of unexplained events. These ghost events have scared many through the years: prisoners, soldiers, settlers, and even recent visitors.

GHOST TOUR INFORMATION		
Month	Departure Times	Cost
May	6:00 p.m. & 8:00 p.m.	$26.50 (adult); $15.00 (child); $75.00 (family)
June-July	5:30 p.m. & 7:30 p.m.	$26.50 (adult); $15.00 (child); $75.00 (family)
August	6:00 p.m. & 8:00 p.m.	$26.50 (adult); $15.00 (child); $75.00 (family)
September	6:30 p.m. & 8:30 p.m.	$26.50 (adult); $15.00 (child); $75.00 (family)
October-April	8:45 p.m. & 9:00 p.m.	$26.50 (adult); $15.00 (child); $75.00 (family)
Tour Duration: Approximately 90 minutes		

Important: Children under 17 must be accompanied by an adult. This tour is not suitable for young children.

Comprehension Check

Check (✓) *True* or *False* for each of the following sentences.

	True	False
1. Over 1,000 people died in the Port Arthur prison.	☐	☐
2. In 1870, Port Arthur offered a lantern-lit ghost tour.	☐	☐
3. Ghost tour visitors tell the guides stories of unexplained events.	☐	☐
4. The ghost tours cost $75 per family and last about 90 minutes.	☐	☐
5. The ghost tours are suitable for participants of all ages.	☐	☐

Reflections   Many aboriginals in Tasmania were killed by the British army and the colonist settlers during the Australian frontier wars. Today, Tasmania's aboriginals own only 2% of the local land. Should more land be given to these original people of Tasmania?

From Crybaby to CR7

Unit Preview

A. Discuss the following questions.

1. Who are some of the greatest football players in the world? What are their nationalities?

2. Do you know any of the football clubs that Cristiano Ronaldo has played for?

3. What do you know about Cristiano Ronaldo the man, not the football player?

B. Match the words with the definitions below. Discuss your answers.

1. _____ mischievous (*adj.*)   a. to carve; to build up

2. _____ humiliate (*v.*)   b. to go away quietly

3. _____ pinnacle (*n.*)   c. a way for someone to express himself or herself

4. _____ outlet (*n.*)   d. playful

5. _____ upbringing (*n.*)   e. the top

6. _____ sneak out (*v.*)   f. to be known as

7. _____ chisel (*v.*)   g. to exceed

8. _____ go by (a name) (*phr.*)   h. unimportant; not connected to something

9. _____ surpass (*v.*)   i. to embarrass

10. _____ irrelevant (*adj.*)   j. the way a child is raised

C. Read the statements and check (✓) *Agree* or *Disagree*. Check the statements again after reading the passage to see whether your opinion has changed.

Statement	Before Reading		After Reading	
	Agree	Disagree	Agree	Disagree
1. Football players love only money, not the game.				
2. Cristiano Ronaldo spends most of his time enjoying his life.				
3. You can be a great football player if you have plenty of natural talent.				

The bronze statue of the football player at the Madeira Airport in Portugal has a mischievous smile on its face. The irony is that as a child, this football player's nickname was "Crybaby." His full name is Cristiano Ronaldo dos Santos Aveiro. These days, Ronaldo goes by a different nickname: CR7.

Cristiano Ronaldo's initials and jersey number are more than a nickname; they represent a sports brand worth over a billion dollars. Ronaldo has over 30 sponsors, and his lifetime contract with Nike is worth close to one billion dollars by itself. On his way to accumulating his fortune, Ronaldo has won every trophy a footballer would put on a personal wish list. How do five **Ballon d'Or**[1], four European Golden Shoes, and 26 team trophies, including five UEFA Champions League titles, sound?

Ronaldo has certainly reached the pinnacle of football fame and fortune. Along the way, his love of the game and desire to win have only been surpassed by his obsessive work ethic. Ronaldo's coaches from Manchester United, Real Madrid, and Juventus will all tell you the same thing: After all the players had finished training and gone home, Ronaldo would head to the gym to chisel his body into the perfect

Cristiano Ronaldo at the FIFA World Cup 2014

Q1

How did Ronaldo reach the pinnacle of fame and fortune?

football machine. This work ethic is what drives him, past the age of 30, to humiliate players in their twenties with his skills, desire to win, and **Adonis-like body**[2]. In comparison, Diego Maradona started doing drugs around the same age.

Go back to his childhood, and you will find a young boy so in love with football that he would sneak out of the house to play it. Perhaps due to his poor upbringing or the death of his alcoholic father, Ronaldo used football as an outlet for something positive in his life. Whatever the reason, Ronaldo played the game with a passion and **work rate**[3] that made his Portuguese teammates call him "Abelhinha" (little bee). Yes, another one of his nicknames.

Add to that "El Commandant" (the Commander), the nickname given to him by the Portuguese national team players. He is literally their captain. Ronaldo once said that the size of his country is irrelevant in football: "We are a small country, but we win great and big competitions." The size of one's desire is what really matters. And Ronaldo's desire gave Portugal its only major football trophy: the 2016 European Championship.

Do you still wonder why Ronaldo was called Crybaby? The reason is that as a boy he cried every time he lost a game. Somehow you get the feeling that CR7 will not be crying anymore.

A bust of Cristiano Ronaldo with a mischievous smile on his face

What is the thing that really matters in football competitions?

TIP

When Are Quotation Marks Used?

Quotation marks are frequently used in writing. Their main use is to indicate someone's exact words (reported speech). One example of reported speech from the previous passage is the sentence "We are a small country, but we win great and big competitions." The quotations tell us that Ronaldo said these words exactly as they are written. Quotations are also used when introducing nicknames. In the previous passage, Ronaldo's nicknames are shown in quotations. Read the following example sentences to better understand the use of quotations: His friends called him "Smiley" because he was always optimistic. His favorite expression was "No worries, be happy!"

---

1 **Ballon d'Or** French for "Golden Ball," the name of the most prestigious football award in Europe. The trophy is given yearly to the best player in Europe for that year.

2 **Adonis-like body** Adonis is an extremely handsome man from Greek mythology. An "Adonis-like body" is a body with perfectly defined muscles and perfect proportions.

3 **work rate** the amount of effort that a player puts into a game

Reading Comprehension

Main Idea • **1. What is the passage mainly about?**

    a. the reason Portugal won the 2016 European Championship

    b. the reasons behind Ronaldo's success

    c. the personal worth of Ronaldo and the CR7 sports brand

    d. the individual and team trophies won by Ronaldo

Detail • **2. Which of the following is true about Ronaldo?**

    a. He has won four Ballon d'Or Awards.   b. His best quality is his desire to win.

    c. He comes from a rich family.   d. He is at the top of football fame and fortune.

Reference • **3. What does the word <u>itself</u> in paragraph 2 refer to?**

    a. Nike   b. Ronaldo

    c. the contract   d. the sports brand

Detail • **4. Which of the following is NOT true about Ronaldo?**

    a. His father died when he was young.

    b. He is obsessed with humiliating football players.

    c. He sneaked out of the house to play football.

    d. As a boy, he cried every time he lost a game.

Vocabulary • **5. Which of the following words is closest in meaning to the word drives in paragraph 3?**

    a. allows   b. motivates   c. asks   d. forces

Inference • **6. What does paragraph 3 suggest about Ronaldo?**

    a. His desire to win is stronger than Maradona's.

    b. His love of the game is stronger than Maradona's.

    c. His football skills are better than Maradona's.

    d. His work ethic is better than Maradona's.

Inference • **7. What does paragraph 5 imply about desire?**

    a. It is the most important thing in football.

    b. It is irrelevant in football.

    c. It is very important when you play for a big country.

    d. It is not important when you are Cristiano Ronaldo.

Summarizing Information

A. Read the passage again. Then, complete the outline below. Use the words in the box.

trophy	upbringing	sneak out	sponsors	desire to win
worth	nickname	work ethic	mischievous	

Ronaldo made his fame and fortune thanks to his love of the game, his ¹_____, and most importantly, his obsessive ²_____.

Childhood	Career	Present
a. Ronaldo's ³_____ was "Crybaby."	a. Ronaldo's personal brand is ⁶_____ over one billion dollars.	a. Ronaldo's bronze statue has a ⁸_____ smile on its face.
b. He would ⁴_____ of the house to play football.	b. He led Portugal to its only major football ⁷_____.	b. He has over 30 ⁹_____.
c. He had a poor ⁵_____.		

B. Complete the summary below with your own words.

Cristiano Ronaldo has loved the game of football ever since ❶_____.
Football may have given young Ronaldo a chance to forget his ❷_____ and the death of ❸_____. Ronaldo's ❹_____ has been even more important to his success than his love of the game. Throughout his career, Ronaldo has won every trophy on a football player's ❺_____. Even today, Ronaldo outshines much younger players with his ❻_____, his desire to win, and his ❼_____. He is the captain of the Portuguese national team, who won its only ❽_____ thanks to his leadership and abilities. Ronaldo is not slowing down either. He is continuing his obsessive gym workouts in order to ❾_____ into the perfect football machine. Ronaldo is truly a world-class player at the top of football ❿_____.

Vocabulary in Context

irony   accumulated   wish list   bronze   Adonis-like   chisel

1. After winning a _____ medal at the Olympics, Jenny retired from professional competition.

2. Bodybuilders constantly _____ their bodies in preparation for competitions.

3. Please tell Dad to put a new smartphone on my birthday _____.

4. A police station is robbed: this is an example of _____.

5. During his life, John D. Rockefeller _____ the largest fortune in modern history.

6. Hugh Jackman is one of those actors with _____ bodies.

1. Students today study too much. They need an _____ for fun in their lives.

   a. obsession   b. outlet

2. Tim's _____ kept him up at night before a big game.

   a. football skills   b. desire to win

3. Every athlete hopes to get a _____ with a major sports company.

   a. contract   b. brand

	Positive	Negative
1. Timmy is <u>obsessive</u> about not sharing his possessions with anyone.	☐	☐
2. Mafia leader Joseph Bonanno rose to the <u>pinnacle</u> of organized crime in America.	☐	☐

Compound Nouns	Your Sentence
1. wish list (= a list of desired things)	*A 9 a.m. to 11 p.m. job is not on my **wish list**.*
2. work ethic (= a belief in the moral value of hard work)	
3. work rate (= the amount of effort shown in a game)	

Read the following description of Cristiano Ronaldo's workout schedule and daily diet routine. Then, do the exercises.

🎧 26

Cristiano Ronaldo works out in the gym 5 days a week for 3-4 hours on each of these days. He rests on Tuesdays and Saturdays. He also gets 8 hours of sleep a night, allowing his body to recover after exercising. These workouts come in addition to the training he does with his football team. Diet is a huge part of his exercise philosophy. He eats 6 small meals a day, separated by intervals of 2-4 hours. His meals include protein, vegetables, and supplements such as vitamins. Sugars are avoided. The table below summarizes his daily diet routine.

Cristiano Ronaldo's Daily Diet Routine

Breakfast	Lunch	Snack	Dinner
Whole-wheat or whole-grain cereal, egg whites, and fruit juice	Whole-wheat pasta, green vegetables, baked potato, and chicken with salad	Tuna roll with fruit juice such as lemon juice	Rice, chicken, or turkey breast, beans and fruits

Comprehension Check
Check (✓) *True* or *False* for each of the following sentences.

	True	False
1. Ronaldo trains with his football team 5 days a week for 3-4 hours.	☐	☐
2. On Tuesdays and Sundays, Ronaldo exercises in the gym.	☐	☐
3. Ronaldo's diet allows his body to recover after exercising.	☐	☐
4. Ronaldo's meals include protein, vegetables, and moderate amounts of sugar.	☐	☐
5. Pork and beef are not part of Ronaldo's daily diet.	☐	☐

Reflections   Professional football players start training at very young ages—sometimes when they are 3 or 4. They then go through many years of hard training until they launch their careers in their late teens. But to make it as pro players, they often give up school and do not have a well-rounded education. Is a career in sports worth not having a proper education in life?

An American
Visionary

Unit Preview

A. Discuss the following questions.

1. Who are some of the great American people you know and admire?

2. You may know these brands: Gucci, Dolce & Gabbana, Chanel, Armani, and DKNY. But do you know the people who started them? How about their nationalities?

B. Match the words with the definitions below. Discuss your answers.

1. _____ vision (*n.*)

2. _____ signature (*adj.*)

3. _____ native (*n.*)

4. _____ visionary (*n.*)

5. _____ bold (*adj.*)

6. _____ fine-tune (*v.*)

7. _____ envision (*v.*)

8. _____ retain (*v.*)

9. _____ empire (*n.*)

10. _____ attempt (*n.*)

a. a person who was born in a certain place

b. a person who has unique ideas for the future

c. characteristic

d. to imagine; to visualize

e. courageous

f. to continue to have something

g. a group of companies controlled by one person

h. to make adjustments

i. the power of imagination

j. the act of trying to achieve something

C. Read the statements and check (✔) *Agree* or *Disagree*. Check the statements again after reading the passage to see whether your opinion has changed.

Statement	Before Reading		After Reading	
	Agree	Disagree	Agree	Disagree
1. It is okay to change your name before you turn 20.				
2. Successful people trust and follow their instincts.				
3. People buy a product because of its brand image.				

You know the name Ralph Lauren. You may have even bought clothes designed by this great American visionary. And if you have not, you have probably seen his creations in shops or online stores. What you may not know is how Ralph Lauren's vision turned a necktie into a fashion empire that reaches across the world.

Ralph Lauren never sold you fashion. What he sold you is his idea of the lifestyle you would like to have. If you ever bought his signature Polo shirt, you bought a dream. And that dream is the hope that the lifestyle envisioned by Ralph Lauren could somehow become yours. According to Ralph Lauren, that lifestyle is all about style: "My symbol was always a polo player because I liked sports, and polo has a stylishness to it. It's all about creating a dream I'd want for myself."

This American visionary was born Ralph Lifshitz in the Bronx, New York, in 1939. He was the youngest of four children. While only a teenager, Ralph changed his last name to Lauren and took his first bold attempts at fashion design. In those early years, he caught the attention

Q1
How did Ralph Lauren catch the attention of Calvin Klein?

of Calvin Klein by wearing a combination of army **fatigues**[1] and tweeds on the Bronx streets. Calvin Klein, also a Bronx native, remembers seeing that strangely dressed kid on the neighborhood streets.

At 26, Ralph Lauren designed a wide European-style necktie and sold it to the Neiman Marcus and Bloomingdale's department stores. Five years later, he opened a Polo clothing boutique on Rodeo Drive in Beverly Hills. His Polo shop offered a whole line of fashion designs. The Rodeo Drive opening made him the first American designer with a freestanding shop.

Ralph Lauren's classic symbol: a polo player on horseback

His fashion empire generated over 6 billion dollars in revenue in 2018, pushing Lauren's personal worth close to 9 billion dollars. Ralph Lauren has translated his vision into success for one simple reason: He understands his customers and sells them a stylish dream. He has also stayed true to what he wants. According to Oprah Winfrey, Ralph Lauren shares her own life philosophy: "Trust instinct to move you forward, know what you want to achieve and then stick to it, and retain a sense of gratitude that can't be faked."

Models walking the runway in Ralph Lauren outfits

Also in 2018, Ralph Lauren celebrated the 50th anniversary of his fashion brand. And though he is no longer the CEO of his company, he is still its executive chairman and chief creative officer. Presently, Ralph Lauren is still working hard at fine-tuning his unique vision.

Q2

What is the personal worth of Ralph Lauren?

TIP

What Is a Biographical Narrative?

The passage above is a biographical narrative. A biographical narrative is a personal story that is often told in chronological sequence (time order). Some biographical narratives are essay-sized or shorter and focused on a topic. Others are as long as books and encompass the entire life of a person. "An American Visionary" is a short biographical narrative. The passage progresses with each paragraph from Ralph Lauren's teenage years to the present day. Throughout the passage, focus is maintained on Ralph Lauren's visionary spirit.

---

1   **fatigues** the uniform worn by a soldier

Reading Comprehension

Main Idea

1. What is the passage mainly about?

a. how the Polo brand got started

b. how the Polo brand became recognized all over the world

c. how Ralph Lauren translated his vision into reality

d. how Ralph Lauren became a billionaire

Detail

2. Which of the following is true about Ralph Lauren?

a. He is the CEO of his company.

b. He is the chief creative officer of his company.

c. He never liked sports.

d. He never thought polo was a stylish sport.

Reference

3. What does the word <u>it</u> in paragraph 5 refer to?

a. your passion   b. your success

c. your gratitude   d. your lifestyle

Detail

4. Which of the following is NOT true about Ralph Lauren?

a. He opened a store on Rodeo Drive.

b. He is a European designer.

c. He is from the Bronx.

d. He was born Ralph Lifshitz.

Vocabulary

5. What does the word line in paragraph 4 mean?

a. a queue   b. a row   c. a border   d. a range

Inference

6. What does paragraph 2 suggest that Ralph Lauren is selling?

a. the sporty image of a polo player   b. stylish clothes

c. an image of a lifestyle that people desire   d. expensive clothes

Inference

7. What does the last paragraph suggest about Ralph Lauren?

a. He has realized his vision.

b. He is abandoning his vision.

c. He is completely changing his vision.

d. He is continuing to refine his vision.

Summarizing Information

A. Read the passage again. Then, complete the outline below. Use the words in the box.

attention   freestanding   stick to   generated   creations   native
signature   visionary   executive chairman   boutique   dream   fine-tuning

Paragraph 1: a. Ralph Lauren is an American [1]_____.

b. His [2]_____ are sold in shops and online stores.

Paragraph 2: a. Ralph Lauren is selling a [3]_____.

b. His [4]_____ design is the Polo shirt.

Paragraph 3: a. Ralph Lauren caught the [5]_____ of Calvin Klein.

b. Calvin Klein was also a Bronx [6]_____.

Paragraph 4: a. Ralph Lauren was the first American designer with a [7]_____ shop.

b. He opened a clothing [8]_____ on Rodeo Drive.

Paragraph 5: a. Ralph Lauren's philosophy is to [9]_____ what he wants to do.

b. In 2018, his company [10]_____ over $6 billion in revenue.

Paragraph 6: a. Ralph Lauren keeps [11]_____ his vision.

b. He is still the [12]_____ of his company.

B. Complete the summary below with your own words.

Ralph Lauren is an American visionary who has brought his vision to people ❶_____.
Ralph Lauren tested his designs on the ❷_____, where he wore striking outfits, such
as a combination of ❸_____. He later sold a ❹_____
to Neiman Marcus and Bloomingdale's. Ralph Lauren followed that success by opening a
❺_____ on Rodeo Drive. He went on to build ❻_____
that stretches across the world. In 2018, Ralph Lauren's company ❼_____ of
over 6 billion dollars. Ralph Lauren is ❽_____ CEO. However, as its chief creative
officer, he continues to work hard at ❾_____.

Vocabulary in Context

A. The box below has words/phrases from the passage. Use them to complete the following sentences.

philosophy   line   move forward   symbol   gratitude   worth

1. The children felt a sense of .... when they were given their Christmas gifts.

2. In order to ...., we need to work better as a team.

3. A new .... of swimsuits will be released at the fashion show.

4. His lifetime .... added up to a few dollars and some used furniture.

5. Chef Brionne's cooking .... is simple: "fresher ingredients, better food."

6. Top Life Insurance stopped using Snoopy as its company ....

B. Choose the correct words/phrases from the passage to complete the sentences below.

1. We are often told to trust our .... when faced with a tough choice in life.

    a. instincts   b. vision

2. Our basketball team .... countless hours of practice into a deserved win.

    a. moved forward   b. translated

3. Sometimes in life, people must .... their beliefs regardless of the consequences.

    a. envision   b. stay true to

C. Determine the connotation (positive or negative meaning) of the underlined words.

	Positive	Negative
1. The murderer's <u>signature</u> method of killing was to slash the throats of his victims.	☐	☐
2. The hacking community continues to <u>fine-tune</u> their methods of attack.	☐	☐

D. Use the following adjectives from the passage to write sentences in the box below.

Adjectives	Your Sentence
1. signature (= characteristic)	*Michael Jackson's **signature** dance move was the moonwalk.*
2. unique (= special)	
3. stylish (= fashionable)	
4. bold (= courageous)	

Reading Connections

Read the following excerpts from a letter from Ralph Lauren to his employees upon his resignation as CEO. Then, do the exercises.

🎧 28

Dear Employees,

Yesterday we made an important announcement, which I believe is the right decision to bring our Company into the future. The Ralph Lauren Corporation is the company I founded, nurtured, and love. I am not stepping down, nor am I stepping back.

My passion for beauty, for authenticity, and for creating timeless, classic products that people all over the world want as part of their lives is what drives me today. As always, each of you plays a role in bringing these dreams to life. Your creativity, hard work, and loyalty have always inspired me, and I am excited to continue working with you as we move forward.

As the Company has grown globally, it has been clear to me that we needed to add strength. I have waited for the right moment to make someone CEO, and I am confident that Stefan Larsson will be a wonderful business partner to help carry out this shared vision. As the largest shareholder, I will continue to nurture and grow this Company. You have my deepest commitment on that.

With warmest regards,

Ralph Lauren

Comprehension Check
Check (✓) *True* or *False* for each of the following sentences.

	True	False
1. Ralph Lauren is informing his employees that he is stepping back.	☐	☐
2. Ralph Lauren is still driven by his passion for beauty and authenticity.	☐	☐
3. Ralph Lauren believes his company must strengthen as it moves forward.	☐	☐
4. Ralph Lauren and Stefan Larsson have different visions about the future.	☐	☐
5. Ralph Lauren will continue to nurture and grow his company as a CEO.	☐	☐

Reflections   If you had the chance to meet Ralph Lauren, what is the one question that you would really want to ask him?